"Scribbling Women"

TRUE TALES FROM ASTONISHING LIVES

Marthe Jocelyn

TUNDRA BOOKS

Published in Canada by Tundra Books,
75 Sherbourne Street, Toronto, Ontario M5A 2P9

Published in the United States by Tundra Books of Northern New York,
P.O. Box 1030, Plattsburgh, New York 12901

Library of Congress Control Number: 2010928788

Library and Archives Canada Cataloguing in Publication

Scribbling women : true tales from astonishing lives / by Marthe Jocelyn.

Includes bibliographical references.
ISBN 978-0-88776-952-8

1. Literature—Women authors.
2. Women authors—Biography. I. Jocelyn, Marthe

PN6069.W65S37 2011   808.8'99287   C2010-903162-8

We acknowledge the financial support of the Government of Canada through the Book Publishing Industry Development Program (BPIDP) and that of the Government of Ontario through the Ontario Media Development Corporation's Ontario Book Initiative. We further acknowledge the support of the Canada Council for the Arts and the Ontario Arts Council for our publishing program.

ONTARIO ARTS COUNCIL
CONSEIL DES ARTS DE L'ONTARIO

Printed and bound in Canada

ANCIENT FOREST
FRIENDLY

This book is printed on acid-free paper that is 100% recycled,
ancient-forest friendly (100% post-consumer waste).

1 2 3 4 5 6   16 15 14 13 12 11

For Kathy

CONTENTS

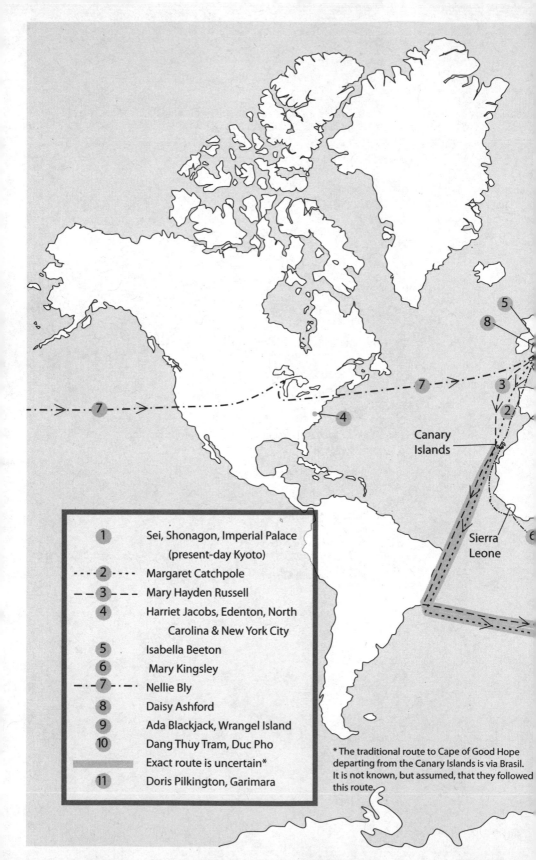

Canary
Islands

Sierra
Leone

1 Sei, Shonagon, Imperial Palace
   (present-day Kyoto)
2 - - - Margaret Catchpole
3 – – – Mary Hayden Russell
4 Harriet Jacobs, Edenton, North
   Carolina & New York City
5 Isabella Beeton
6 Mary Kingsley
7 –·–·– Nellie Bly
8 Daisy Ashford
9 Ada Blackjack, Wrangel Island
10 Dang Thuy Tram, Duc Pho
   Exact route is uncertain*
11 Doris Pilkington, Garimara

* The traditional route to Cape of Good Hope
departing from the Canary Islands is via Brasil.
It is not known, but assumed, that they followed
this route.

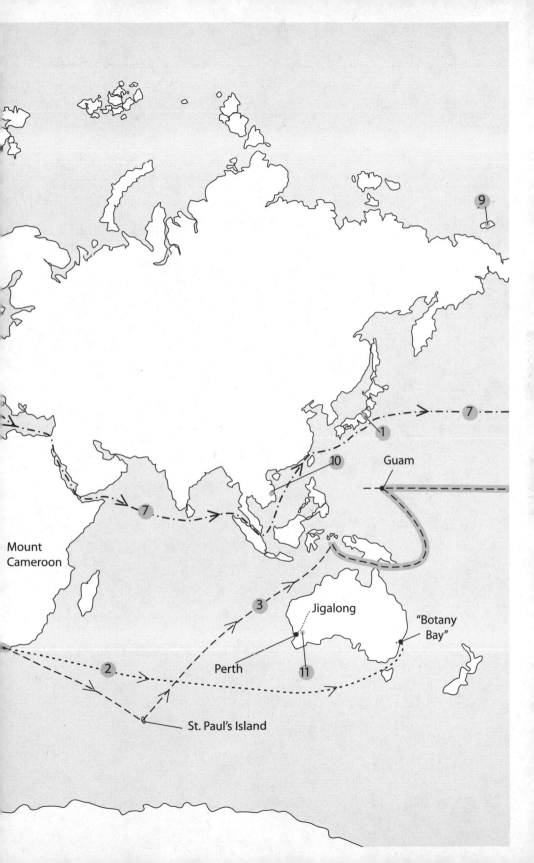

To Begin

I like to write outside, at a table on my front porch, or even in the hammock. Sometimes I sit on a park bench and scribble away while I watch the world around me. Once in a while, I stay in bed on a cold winter morning, with a hot water bottle, a cup of tea, and a notebook across my knees

I am a professional writer. I write books for young readers and get paid for it. Occasionally I have a worrisome deadline or a computer glitch that causes a few stormy hours, but that's as awful as my writing life gets. I am lucky to have a job that changes every time I turn a page, that allows me to read books, look at art, wander through the streets, travel afar, talk to and eavesdrop on people . . . all in the name of research.

Whether I'm writing a book of information, like this one, or making up a story with entirely fictional characters, part of every day is spent in research. Reading about one thing inevitably uncovers fascinating details about something else, and I love to follow where curiosity leads me.

This happened while I was working on a book called *A Home for Foundlings,* about a centuries-old institution in England that rescued hundreds of abandoned children. As I delved into that topic, I came across the letters of Lady Mary Wortley Montagu, wife of the ambassador to Turkey nearly three hundred years ago. In one of her many letters she described the common practice of inoculation against smallpox performed by the Turks. In England, where this dreadful disease was killing one person in six, Lady Mary's observations were a crucial step toward ending the smallpox epidemic. The foundlings were used, with no ill effect, in medical experiments—the first recorded instance of what we now know as clinical trials—to help doctors determine the correct procedure and dosage to use on the general population.

As I learned and thought about Lady Mary's life, I realized that there must be dozens of other women who had written letters, or travel journals, or essays, or diaries; women whose observations, like Lady Mary's, had chronicled or changed the world around them, even in very small ways.

A quick search in the library and on the Internet told me there were not dozens, but *thousands* of women who had recorded their lives—joyful, challenging, illuminating, wearisome, and passionate—on *countless* pages, throughout history and around the world.

Limited by language, I looked only at texts written, or translated into, English. There were still more words written by women than I could read in a lifetime. The trouble was not where to begin but where to stop. Finally the list was narrowed to those whose stories made me catch my breath.

The physical act of writing intrigued me: where and when had these girls and women found time to put words down on paper? A few of my subjects depended on writing for part of their livelihood, but most of them had plenty else to consume their days, from waiting on royalty to surviving blizzards, stealing horses, delivering babies, visiting cannibal tribes, performing surgery in a war zone . . . and so much more.

In some cases, the discovery or preservation of a particular journal or manuscript is a key part of the tale. Today's electronic correspondence is fast and convenient, but it leaves us with nothing to hold on to. Even if we are somehow able to read e-mails two or three hundred years from now, there will not be the tangible connection of fingering a lock of hair or a scrap of flannel pinned to the edge of a diary page, where every third or fourth word required the pen to be dipped again into the ink, or the pencil to be sharpened.

Most of "my" women would be surprised to find themselves inside a book. They might not be surprised, however, to know that the title began as a sneer, made by a famous male writer named Nathaniel Hawthorne in a letter to his publisher in 1855, where he complained about what he considered the irritating fad of "scribbling women."

Everyone has trials and sorrows, and moments of boredom or immense delight. But these scribbling women wrote it down, passed it along, told us they were here, and took the time to illuminate their worlds.

For us, their grateful readers.

Sei Shonagon

965–1010

I really can't understand people who get angry when they hear gossip about others. How can you not discuss other people? Apart from your own concerns, what can be more beguiling to talk about and criticize than other people?

～

How can you not discuss other people? We all do it.

There is simply nothing more fascinating to people than other people. This has been true for at least a thousand years. The words above were written in the tenth century, by a lady-in-waiting in the imperial court of Japan.

We know her by the name of Sei Shonagon, but that would not have been what she was called. Sei was her family name, and the word *shonagon* meant "junior counsellor," probably the job of one of her male relatives. Some scholars think her personal name was Nagiko, but here she'll be referred to as Sei.

Sei's masterwork, called in English *The Pillow Book,* is not a memoir, nor a diary, nor poetry, but in a way it is all of these. Written in snippets during ten years at the royal court, *The Pillow Book* is a collection of lists, anecdotes, poems, gossip, reminiscences, and astute observations of the people and rituals that Sei encountered each day.

Sei was born in the year 965 CE. She arrived at court in her mid-twenties to serve Sadako, the first wife of the Emperor Ichijo. The routine life of the women in the palace had much to do with appearing lovely, preparing the tea ceremony, and providing witty conversation and entertainment for each other, as well as for the men.

The identity of Sei's mother is unknown, but her father and grand-father were both famous poets in Japan during this time called the Heian period. *Heian* means something close to "peace and tranquility." Art, poetry, and literature were particularly prized by the Japanese nobility. Educated Japanese men prided themselves on writing in Chinese, a language forbidden to the women. Instead, the women wrote with a collection of symbols called *hiragana,* using a brush and ink. No one had ever written a book like Sei's—in any language—so there is no way of guessing what inspired her to make her mark in so unusual a way.

All we really know about Sei is what she revealed in her own book. She was fiercely opinionated, sharp-eyed, and ruthless in her descriptions of other courtiers. She was quick-witted and flirtatious, with two main passions: she adored her Empress with unfaltering admiration, and she prized poetry above almost anything else.

However critical Sei may have been of her fellow courtiers, her book often describes Empress Sadako's beauty and exquisite kimonos: "Where else would one ever see a red Chinese robe like this? Beneath it she wore a willow-green robe of Chinese damask, five layers of unlined robes of grape-colored silk, a robe of Chinese gauze with blue prints over a plain white background, and a ceremonial skirt of elephant-eye silk. I felt that nothing in the world could compare with the beauty of these colors."

Sei was miffed when Sadako showed a momentary preference for anyone other than Sei, but delighted and gratified when she was clearly the favorite. The women often teased or complimented each other through impromptu poems, like this one:

> *The years have passed*
> *And age has come my way.*
> *Yet I need only look at this fair flower*
> *For all my cares to melt away.*

Just as text messages are a common form of communication between friends and sweethearts today, the exchange of poetry was how word got around in Sei's life at court. A servant could be ordered (at any time of the day or night) to provide paper and ink for composition, and then to carry a poem to someone else in the palace. The choice of paper was a kind of declaration; its weight and color were clues to the feelings of the sender. Sei often mentioned—sometimes critically— what the poem *looked* like, as well as the words it contained. In her list of "Unsuitable Things," for instance, she mentions "Ugly handwriting on red paper."

The setting that Sei reveals is as foreign to the modern Western reader as the world of a fantasy novel. But inside the ancient and exotic Emperor's palace, thanks to Sei's illumination, the people—the women in particular—are shown to share feelings and flaws that are utterly familiar, like those remarks about gossiping.

Altogether, *The Pillow Book* consists of about 320 pieces, half of which are lists. Here is a sampling of the lists and some of what she included under each evocative title:

Things that can't be compared
Night and day.
Laughter and anger.
Old age and youth.
The man you love and the same man once you've lost all
    feeling for him seem like two completely different people.

Things that Pass by Rapidly
A boat with its sail up.
People's age.
Spring. Summer. Autumn. Winter.

Scruffy Things
The back of a piece of embroidery.
The inside of a cat's ear.

Occasions for Anxious Waiting
You become very anxious when you have to make a quick

response to someone's poem, and you can't come up with
anything.

Elegant Things
A white coat worn over a violet waistcoat.
Duck eggs.
Plum blossoms covered with snow.
A pretty child eating strawberries.

Things That Make Me Happy
I know I shouldn't think this way, and I know I'll be punished
for it, but I just love it when bad things happen to people I
can't stand.

Hateful Things
Very hateful is a mouse that scurries all over the place.
One is just about to be told some interesting piece of news when
    a baby starts crying.
A person who recites a spell himself after sneezing. In fact I
    detest anyone who sneezes, except the master of the house.

Another hateful thing, according to Sei, was when someone's poetry was not admirable: "I particularly despise people who express themselves poorly in writing. . . . It's bad enough to receive poorly written letters oneself, and just as disgraceful when they're sent to others . . ." But she also exults, "If letters did not exist, what dark depressions would come over one! . . . a letter really seems like an elixir of life."

Sei recorded her own witticisms in an almost gloating tone. She was quick to pass harsh judgment on everyone's behavior and appearance and often had spats or rivalries with both men and women whom she deemed in some way unworthy.

A reference to Sei appears in the diary of another woman who achieved fame as a writer during this era. Lady Murasaki Shikibu wrote a romantic novel called *The Tale of Genji*. She described Sei this way: "Sei

Shonagon has the most extraordinary air of self-satisfaction. . . . She is a gifted woman, to be sure. Yet, if one gives free rein to one's emotions even under the most inappropriate circumstances, if one has to sample each interesting thing that comes along, people are bound to regard one as frivolous. And how can things turn out well for such a woman?"

Sei's beloved Empress Sadako died two days after giving birth, in the year 1000. Sei withdrew from court and there is no further trustworthy information about what happened to her. One story says that she died alone and very poor, but that may have been a rumor circulated by her rivals.

What we do know is that her collection of words, her "scribbles," have lasted centuries more than most writers ever dream of, making the following lines true indeed.

> . . . if I happen to come by some lovely white paper for every day use and a good writing brush . . . I'm immensely cheered, and find myself thinking I might perhaps be able to go on living for a while longer after all.

Sei Shonagon's notes were delivered within minutes of writing them—almost like e-mail. And if she did not receive a reply at once, she twitched with irritation.

Margaret Catchpole's letters took months to arrive at their destination, and she could never be certain whether she'd hear any answer at all . . .

Margaret Catchpole

1762–1819

ipswich may 25th 1801

i am sorrey I have to inform you this Bad newes that I am a going a way on wedensday next or Thursday at the Longest so I hav taken the Libberty my good Lady of trobling you with a few Lines as it will Be the Larst time I ever Shall trobell you in this Sorrofoll Confinement my sorrowes are very grat to think I must Be Bannished out of my owen Countreay and from all my Dearest friends for ever . . .

Margaret Catchpole wrote this letter from prison, where she had been waiting to learn the punishment for her crime of stealing a horse. She had just heard the worst possible news. She was not to be hanged, as she had hoped, but instead would be transported away from her homeland of England for the remainder of her life, to a distant place now known as Australia.

Crime affected nearly everyone who lived in England during the eighteenth century, especially in the towns and cities. The capital city of London was bursting with new arrivals from the countryside, all struggling to stay alive by whatever means they could among the gin stalls, dark alleys, and rat-infested lodgings. Survival sometimes meant stealing and cheating, or worse.

Margaret came from a tiny seaside village, but, like thousands of others seeking a fortune, she traveled to London when she had something to sell—in this case, the very horse she had stolen and ridden to get there!

Margaret had grown up poor and unschooled on the farms where her father worked as a ploughman. During those years, she'd learned to ride a horse with great confidence. She was a servant in several homes before being hired by the Cobbold family. It was Mrs. Cobbold who taught her to read and write a little, between helping with the children and the kitchen chores.

There is now great suspicion about the legend of Margaret's daring deeds, but even the facts that can be checked tell quite a story. Her first biographer was the Reverend Richard Cobbold, little Dick, son of Margaret's employer. His book was called *History of Margaret Catchpole, a Suffolk Girl*. It is the Reverend Cobbold's fault that Margaret's true history is so unclear. He recognized that his family had been close to a notorious celebrity and he could not resist adding a number of fictional episodes, characters, and motives to his account of her life.

He gave her credit for having rescued various Cobbold children from terrible accidents—according to him, she shielded two from a falling wall, and saved another from drowning. But the first certain drama in Margaret's life took place when she was fourteen. She galloped bareback for nine miles to fetch a doctor for her ailing mistress, causing astonishment throughout the county. It was not the same horse that later got her into trouble, but it was the same skill as a rider.

After many years of loyal service, in 1795 Margaret stopped working for the Cobbolds. She was thirty-three years old. Nearly two years later, she stole their horse, "which she rode from thence to London in about 10 hours dressed in a man's apparel, [and] having offered it for sale she was detected."

The Reverend Cobbold's book claimed that Margaret was under the influence of a scoundrel sweetheart named Will Laud, but that romance cannot be proved as fact. Having lived in a town beside the ocean, where smuggling was a common trade, it is possible that Margaret was acquainted with seedy characters, but not necessarily in love with one of them. However, she'd always been a "good" girl, hard-working and loyal. When such a person performs a desperate and foolish deed, the obvious question is, "Was this for love?" We'll never know.

At the time of Margaret's crime, there was not yet an official police force, so the court system was clogged with troublemakers of all kinds. Back then there were severe penalties for offenses we would consider minor today. Two hundred crimes were punishable by hanging! Apart from the serious crimes, like murder, arson, and highway robbery, some of the milder offenses were: pilfering anything worth more than five shillings, such as a hat, a lady's slip, or a piece of meat; picking someone's pocket of a silk handkerchief or wallet; and—as Margaret had discovered—stealing any sort of animal. All this meant that the jails were dangerously crowded, dingy, and awful-smelling, as well as teeming with contagious diseases. Officials were forced to consider alternative methods of punishment.

The explorer James Cook recommended to the British government that the remote Botany Bay he'd discovered in 1770 would make an ideal destination for surplus prisoners. The actual settlement was along the coast from Cook's original site, but to this day, the phrase "Botany Bay" is synonymous with banishment to a bleak land full of rough characters.

Margaret was held for three long years in a local jail while awaiting the ship that would carry her away from England. The idea of traveling to an unknown land must have frightened the sense right out of her head, because in March of 1800, Margaret staged a daring escape from the Ipswich prison. She climbed up and over a twenty-two-foot-high spiked fence to freedom. But a week later she was recaptured, "dressed in a sailor's habit, and safely conducted back to her old compartment."

Imprisoned until August, "she again received the death sentence but [was] reprieved before the Judge left the town." She may have felt more

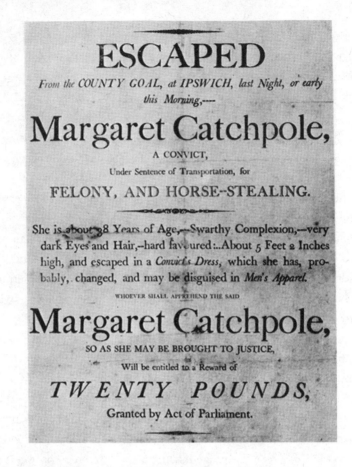

ESCAPED

From the COUNTY GOAL, at IPSWICH, last Night, or early
this Morning,----

Margaret Catchpole,

A CONVICT,

Under Sentence of Transportation, for

FELONY, AND HORSE--STEALING.

She is about 38 Years of Age,--Swarthy Complexion,--very
dark Eyes and Hair,--hard favoured:..About 5 Feet 2 Inches
high, and escaped in a *Convict's Dress*, which she has, probably,. changed, and may be disguised in *Men's Apparel.*

WHOEVER SHALL APPREHEND THE SAID

Margaret Catchpole,

SO AS SHE MAY BE BROUGHT TO JUSTICE,

Will be entitled to a Reward of

TWENTY POUNDS,

Granted by Act of Parliament.

cursed than lucky to have had her penalty reduced to Transportation
for Life.

The courts had been exiling people to Australia since a convoy
of eleven ships, known as the First Fleet, had sailed from England in
1787, carrying nearly 800 convicts. Altogether, during eighty years of
Transportation, more than 162,000 criminals became the pioneers of
this huge unknown continent. The human cargo was accompanied by
cows, sheep, goats, hogs, chickens, and five rabbits. This menagerie was
intended to supply ongoing generations, just as the people were.

Finally, in May of 1801, with ninety-five other female prisoners,
Margaret departed from home on a ship called the *Nile.* One hundred
and seventy-six days later (a trip that today takes about seventeen hours

by airplane), she disembarked, just before Christmas, in Sydney Cove on the other side of the world. The colony must have seemed as fearfully different from England as the moon might be—but even farther away: "At least one could see the moon from England."

The conditions on board the *Nile* had certainly been grim, making the sight of land—even such a strange land—a joyous relief. The settlers already in residence would have been just as excited to greet the new arrivals. A ship meant letters from home, even if the news was nine months old. There was a war going on in Europe, where a cocky French general named Napoleon Bonaparte was taking steps to declare himself emperor. A ship would also bring much-needed supplies as well as fresh workers, servants, and women to a population hardly yet able to support itself with crops and fishing.

Many of the female criminals originally destined to be hanged on the gallows had had their sentences commuted to Transportation because the officials realized there was a desperate need for young women to bear children, to supply future generations for the new colony. Some of these women eagerly paired up with soldiers, handsome in their scarlet uniform jackets, and traded their charms for better treatment or reduced labor time. Margaret Catchpole was past the age when she could provide children, but she found other ways to contribute to the settlement.

The First Fleet convicts had lived in tents or crude cabins, but by the time of Margaret's arrival, thirteen years later, there was a real town with simple cottages for the convicts to live in, most with verandas to shade them from the scorching sun. Bush flies buzzed about constantly and goats and dogs roamed the laneways. Enterprising residents recalled the streets of London by selling oysters or pies from market stalls. After a few years, the convicts were obliged to wear black-and-yellow uniforms to distinguish them from the free settlers, but there was no such need when Margaret was newly landed; almost every European living in Sydney Cove was either a prisoner or a guard.

Although there were no high fences to climb, the inmates of this prison town had no interest in escaping. Fear kept them in place. Margaret's letters often refer to the "savages" who roamed the vast open wilderness beyond the edge of town. When the British had arrogantly claimed this territory for their king, they'd ignored the entire aboriginal population, who had lived there for at least twenty thousand years. Members of the Gweagal clan were the people most immediately affected by the invasion of the pale men in "big canoes," and they were not happy about it.

There were many clashes over the years, with killings on both sides. Certainly the convicts were wary of these "savages" who could throw spears with fatal accuracy. But the white men had even deadlier weapons: first guns, and then smallpox. This disease, carried unintentionally from England, killed countless aborigines.

Margaret's first job in Sydney Cove was as a cook for the commissary, Mr. John Palmer, whose wife later became a good friend to Margaret. Cooking must have been one of the preferred positions, far easier than farm work or building. Had she already shown that her intention to stay out of trouble was more than an idle promise?

Throughout her sentence, Margaret wrote letters to friends and acquaintances back home, though paper was scarce and her spelling was terrible. Why did she choose to write to Mrs. Cobbold, the very woman whose horse she had stolen? Why was she compelled to be in touch with other people who must have seemed like foggy memories as the years sailed by? Being nearly illiterate, why did she write at all?

We are lucky that she did, because the eleven letters that still exist are now considered rare documents and are kept in a museum. It turned out that Margaret was a unique and important witness to the original European colony in Australia. We know certain details thanks only to her scrawls.

On January 21, 1802, after one month of living in the far-away, unfamiliar country, Margaret began her letter to Mrs. Cobbold using these words: "honred madam with grat plesher i take up my penn to a Quaint you, my good Ladday, of my saf a rivel at port Jackson new South Wales sedeny on the 20th Day of Desember 1801 . . ."

Margaret's unschooled spelling sometimes makes her letters difficult to read. Here is a translation:

Honored Madam,

With great pleasure I take up my pen to acquaint you, my
good lady, of my safe arrival at Port Jackson, New South Wales,
Sydney, on the 20th day of December, 1801 . . .

It is possible, reading her words aloud, to hear how her accent might
have sounded, as she likely spelled out the letters the way she heard herself speak.

The first letter goes on to say: " . . . It is a Grat deel moor Lik englent
then ever i Did expet to a seen for hear is Gardden stuff of all koind—
expt gosbres an Currenes and appelles." More clearly spelled, this would
be: "It is a great deal more like England than ever I did expect to have
seen, for here is garden stuff of all kind, except gooseberries and currants and apples . . ."

(For clarity, further transcriptions of Margaret's letters will have the
correct spelling, unless noted.)

It is touching, after all she'd been through, to imagine Margaret
being homesick for something as simple as gooseberries. But the new
world was not entirely gardens and beautiful parrots and pretty woods.
Without giving a reason, she states, in capital letters: "FOR I MUST SAY
THIS IS THE WICKEDEST PLACE I EVER WAS IN ALL MY LIFE."

She is pleased to report that not one woman had died on the voyage,
and that as her work assignment is minimal, she has a fair amount of
freedom, only being expected at a "general muster. Then I must appear
to let them know I am here."

Even in a community of convicts, however, Margaret explained
that those who broke the rules ended up in a worse situation: "They
have their poor head shaved and sent up to the coal river and there carry
coals from day light in the morning till dark at night, and half starved,
but I hear that is a-going to be put by, and so it had need, for it is very
cruel indeed."

In other cases, offenders were banished to an isolated isle off the coast:
"Norfolk Island is a bad place enough to send any poor creature, with steel
collar on their poor necks, but I will take good care of myself from that."

She signed off, "from your unfortunate servant, Margaret Catchpole."

But then, "Madam," she instructed Mrs. Cobbold in a postscript. "Be so kind as to let Doctor Stebbings have that side of the letter . . ."

There was a shortage of paper, but Margaret was resourceful. She used the same piece of paper to write letters to two people, trusting that when one had finished reading, he or she would deliver the note to the other recipient. There was no need to remember any street address, as only the person's name and village were needed to guarantee delivery.

Dr. Stebbings, according to Reverend Cobbold's book, was the doctor to whom Margaret had galloped so many years before, seeking medical aid for her mistress. Whether she had known him quite so long as that, he seems to have been familiar with several inmates at the Ipswich jail, so perhaps he attended them as prison doctor. Margaret reported on other local women who had made the crossing with her: "Barker is alive but she was very much frightened at the 'rufness' of the sea. She used to very often cry out, 'I wish I was with my dear Mr. Stebbens for I never shall see Ipswich no more,' but she is much the same as ever . . ."

Here is Margaret's description (showing the prejudice typical in those days) of the new race of humans she was encountering:

To Dr. Stebbings:

. . . Pray give my best respects to all my old fellow prisoners and tell them never to say 'dead hearted' at the thought of coming to Botany Bay for it is likely you may never see it, for it is not inhabited, only by the blacks, the natives of this place—they are very savage for they always carry with them spears and toma-hawks so when they can meet with a white man they will rob them and spear them. I for my part do not like them. I do not know how to look at them—they are such poor naked creatures. They behave themselves well enough when they come in to my house for if not we would get them punished. They very often have a grand fight with themselves, 20 and 30 all together—and we pray to be spared. Some of them are killed. There is nothing said to them for killing one another.

Relations between the white colonists and the aboriginal people continued to be uneasy and even hostile. Margaret added a postscript in the note to Dr. Stebbings:

> . . . the Blacks, the natives of this place, killed and wounded 8 men and women and children. One man, they cut off his arms half way up and broke the bones that they left on very much, and cut their legs off up to their knees and the poor man was carried in to the hospital alive. But the Governor have sent men out after them to shoot every one they find, so as I hope I shall give you better account the next letter.

The next letter was a long time coming. Margaret and the other convicts depended on ships for their postal service. In one letter she said, "I hope, my good lady, you write to the first transport ship that do come out for I should be very glad to hear from you," and again later, "By this day twelve months I shall be in great hopes of a return of a letter." What she means is that it will be six months before her letter will reach England, and six months for the next ship to come back—*a full year* before she can hope to hear a reply!

In nearly every note, Margaret provides an update on the cost of things, such as tea, sugar, salt beef, mutton, "fifteen shillings for a pair of shoes," fabric, soap, and "fish is as cheap as anything we can buy, but we have no money to trade with here."

The next existing letter is addressed to her Aunt and Uncle Howes, dated December 20, 1804, when there is summer weather in Australia. It was probably written in time to be put on a ship departing for England: "Hoping they are all in good health as it leave me—Bless God for it—and as young as ever and in good spirits I will assure you uncle I should be almost ready to jump over St. John Church, which is the first church that is finished in the country."

She mentioned early on that this is the fourth letter she had sent so far—probably one each year—and named the boats that carried them. She was "hoping that I should have had a letter long before this. Time here is long—it's enough to make me go out of my mind to see so many letters come from London and poor I cannot get not one."

Even so far away, Margaret must have known that her homeland was at war with Napoleon. She told her uncle to think what a "comfort it would be for me to hear from you all, as I hear England is in a very bad state."

New South Wales did not feel much safer: "This is a very dangerous country to live in, for the natives they are black men and women. They go naked. They used to kill the white people very much but they are better—but bad enough—now. The black snakes is very bad for they will fly at you like a dog and if they bite us we die at sundown. Here is some 12 feet long and as big as your thigh."

She went on to say: "I am in great hopes that—please God—I should live so long as 2 or 3 years. I shall have that pleasure and that great joy of seeing you all, for this Governor is a very good man to pardon such as has heavy sentences for life. Here have been a great many that have got their free pardon." She explained that the young man who would be delivering this letter to her aunt and uncle had been a footman in a colonial household where she'd been a dairy maid, both of them convicts. He "was for life but now he is come free to his own home, which is in London."

Being pardoned and released back into the world, to live how and where they chose, was a dream that sustained Margaret and most other prisoners throughout their terms.

The summers were hot, she wrote, and the winters cold, not with snow but "just very white frosts. . . . Here is a few apple and pear trees and grapes, a few oak trees but no other sort except *petches and apery Cot* [peaches and apricot], no gooseberries nor currants." Still missing gooseberries after so many years!

She finished with a blessing: "So I must conclude with all my best prayers and wishes to you all—and I remain your loving cousin."

Enclosed in the letter of 1804 was a separate note to Mrs. Cobbold:

I keep myself free from all men and that is more than any woman can say in the whole colony, young or old—for the young *Gairles* [girls] that are born in this country marry very young at 14 or 15 years old. Everything is very forward in this country—but very uncertain—we may have a good crop of grain on the ground today and all cut off by the next in places, by a hailstorm or a blight or a flood. On Monday last . . . a hailstorm went over in places and cut down the wheat just as it was in bloom. The hail stones was as big as pigeon's eggs. . . .

The natives are not so wicked as they were. They are getting very civil. But will work very little—they say the white man work and the Black man patter—the word patter is eat—they are great creatures to fight amongst themselves with spears . . .

As in nearly every letter, on October 18, 1807 she listed the prices of common necessities:

Shoes 10 and 13 shillings per pair, no linen cloth of no sort to be got, everything very dear indeed, no paper to be got for newspapers. Thread at this time is 1 shilling per skein, but I have a little left of that you sent me in that very nice box. That was a great comfort to me as I had been so very ill at that time and under doctor Mason's care, and about 8 months ago, to oblige Mrs. Palmer, I took a very long walk to 30 miles and overheat myself. I come out with blisters on my back as if I had been burnt by small coals of fire and swelled so bad that I thought I should have been dead very soon. But Bless be to God I did recover.

She went on to ask, "If you have any knowledge of Governor Bligh and can petition to him, there is no doubt but something would be done for me as I behave so well and never get into no trouble." (William Bligh was the fourth governor of New South Wales, but had become notorious when he captained a ship called HMS *Bounty*. His crew staged a mutiny and rebelled against their captain. Captain Bligh, with a few other officers, was set adrift in a small boat and sailed an amazing 3,618 nautical miles to safety.)

Most of the letter written on October 8, 1809, told of a devastating occurrence the previous spring when the Hawkesbury River flooded its banks and destroyed crops and homes for miles. In today's world, the television news makes us all familiar with the destruction from tornados, tsunamis, and hurricanes. Margaret's letter, however, is the only existing eyewitness account of this calamity:

. . . I am almost broken-hearted—first with the floods, 2nd with fear, 3rd with such surprising high winds that cleared acres of standing timber and trees that were of a very great size. We was afraid to stop indoors, my good lady. Here have been a flood in the month of May which distressed us very much. The next flood—on the last day of July and the first day of August—the highest that was ever known by the white men—went over the tops of the houses and many poor creatures crying out for mercy, crying out for boats, firing off gun in distress. It was shocking to hear. This is the second time that one Thomas Lacey, his wife and family, was carried away in their barn. . . . They made holes in the thatch and was taken out by men in boats. . . . Many a one was drowned and at the time the flood was at the height, we all was in great fear we should be starved when the wheat stacks, barns and houses went. Many thousand bushels of Indian corn was washed away. We make bread of that instead of wheat. Most part of the wheat that was in the ground was killed by the flood. . . . I rent a small farm—only 20 acres—but half of it cleared. I live in my little cottage all alone except a little child or two come and stop with me. My good lady, you know I am very fond of children. . . . I should have done very well had not this shocking flood come—it have made me very poor. My loss is about fifty pound and within a very little of loosing my own life by the ground caving away.

One of William Bligh's initial acts as governor was to distribute relief provisions to the farmers hurt by the flood, assistance that would have pleased Margaret.

Richmond Hill September 1ˢᵗ 1811

Honoured Madam, On the 28ᵗʰ of August I received my cedar case that Captain Pritchard should have brought. It is almost 2 years ago since he landed the troops here. Mrs. Palmer my worthy good friend took care of it in her own store room till I could go down myself and when I heard of it I set off and walked all the way down, and it is fifty miles from Richmond Hill to Sidney.

Margaret was appreciative and homesick whenever she received gifts from her former employer: "The cap you sent me off your head was a great comfort to me. I put it on and wear it. I drink the tea with tears and heavy heart."

She says in this letter that although she is nearly fifty, she is still healthy: "i have Lorst all my frunt teeth. i can Stur a Bout as Brisk as ever and in good spirites." Clearly, her spelling never improved. "i am Liven all a Loon as Befor in a very onest way of Life—hear is not one woman in the Coloney Liv Lik my self." Translation: "I am living all alone as before in a very honest way of life. Here is not one woman in the colony live like myself . . ."

It seems to have been the widely accepted custom that everyone find a mate to live with, married or not, perhaps to share costs as well as company. Margaret never married, did not share her little cottage, and never had children of her own. But, learning as she went, she delivered dozens of baby colonists and was so dedicated a nurse and midwife that the maternity ward of Hawkesbury Hospital, Windsor, bears her name. She eventually earned enough money to open a general store in Hawkesbury.

In January of 1814, Margaret heard the long-awaited news that she had been pardoned by William Bligh's replacement, Governor Macquarie, fourteen years into her life sentence. She was fifty-four years old. She was now free, and could have returned to England. Why didn't she go? Would the passage have cost more money than she could put together? Was she afraid of repeating that long, perilous voyage? Had she heard perhaps that Mrs. Cobbold had died?

Or possibly, after so much time, Margaret finally felt that she was at home in New South Wales. Whatever the reason, she stayed there, minding a little shop and delivering babies, until she died of influenza four years later.

In her first letter from the colony Margaret wrote, "I was tossed about very much indeed, but I should not mind it if I was but a-coming to old England once more, for I cannot say that I like this country—no, nor never shall." When had she changed her mind?

Margaret Catchpole crossed about 22,000 ocean miles against her will. She likely spent most of the voyage below decks in misery.

Mary Hayden Russell set out eagerly to sea and was mesmerized by the majesty of the rolling waves—a good thing, because she'd be sailing far from home for more than a year . . .

Mary Hayden Russell

1784–1855

March 18ᵗʰ (1823): The weather being unpleasant had confined me to the cabin all day, but the evening proving fine I had a chair placed on deck to see the sun set. My whole mind was engaged in contemplating the magnificence of the sun, when I heard a scream from my dear little Charles . . .

～

Mary Hayden Russell went to sea in the days when few women left home and women on board ships were considered bad luck. Even women raised in seafaring families on Mary's home island of Nantucket did not normally become sailors. It is hard to guess what gave her the gumption to set out across the ocean, where she encountered ferocious storms, pirates, astonishing islanders, and over forty whales.

Mary's husband was Captain Laban Russell. Her second voyage with him was on the whaling ship *Emily*. Her older son, William, was a boat-steerer on the same vessel. In January 1823, two months before this journal entry, Mary had embarked with her five-year-old son, Charles, the first child to be taken along on such a voyage. What compelled her to exchange a comfortable home for many months in tight quarters with a crew of coarse-talking men? They must have been superstitious about having her with them, and she likely disrupted the rough-and-tumble ways of ship life. In the above entry, Mary used the revealing phrase, "I had a chair placed on deck . . ." reminding us that she did not move the chair herself, being a lady, even under difficult circumstances. And why did she choose to bring a small boy on board a ship that faced daily peril in pursuit of the world's largest mammal?

On that March day when Mary heard her son scream, it turned out that "dear little Charles" had fallen and "snapt" his wrist. "Such an accident on the land would have been distressing," she wrote. "But what were my feelings when I saw the child writhing in agony and no surgeon on board?" Luckily for Charles, his father remained calm, taking him "immediately below and with a man to steady the arm set it and splintered it up."

What we know of Mary's life is only what can be pieced together from this one sample of writing, an extended, journal-like letter that she composed for her married daughter, Mary Ann, aware that her travels would keep her far from a post office. Her account is now part of the collection at the Nantucket Historical Society. Officially recorded dates—of her birth, her marriage, and the births of her children—along with the letter and some guesswork, give us a blurred picture of this unusual woman.

In writing, she never once referred to her husband, Captain Russell, by name, but instead called him either "Captain" or "your dear father."

The first entry was made early in February 1823. The ship was sailing past the Canary Islands shortly after a harrowing gale during which two men were lost overboard. Also torn from their fastenings were the small boats that were essential to the chase and capture of whales.

After pronouncing merely "Alas!" over the drowned men, Mrs. Russell reported with relief that damages to the ship's hull were reparable, and then went on: "The remainder of this eventful night was spent by me in adoring the sparing mercy and goodness of God, who amidst our severe chastenings still had compassion and spared us, tho utterly unworthy, for a little longer. The sea continued to rage with indescribable violence . . ."

Not surprisingly, it is the weather that Mary mentioned most frequently, since shipboard life was entirely dictated by the force and direction of the wind, and the roughness of the sea.

Why were men, let alone women, eager to risk their lives on raging waters in order to hunt whales?

In 1823, when Mary was scribbling her letter, neither electricity nor gas was yet used in homes to provide light or heat for cooking. These essential resources, now taken for granted, were then supplied by whale oil, gathered through the perseverance of a few brave men. From the vantage point of the twenty-first century, the slaughter of many thousands of whales may seem horribly barbaric, but at the time it was a vital contribution to the everyday life of millions of people.

Oil was the main object of the whale hunt; it was used for household lamps, for cooking, and for soap, as well as providing a lubricant for sewing machines and other industry. City streetlights and the enormous lamps in lighthouses were also fueled with oil. Other parts of the whale had functions, too. Whalebone was used to make umbrellas, canes, and corsets—then a fundamental item in every woman's wardrobe. Whale meat was eaten by humans in some areas of the world and by animals elsewhere. A thick substance called ambergris, from the digestive system of the sperm whale, was the most valuable product of all—the crucial ingredient in fine perfume.

As European and American sailors traveled farther from home in search of rich hunting grounds, they encountered ports and islands that they had never dreamed of. They became explorers and ambassadors as well as whalers. Some thought of themselves as conquerors, too, assuming the right to impose the values of home on distant cultures. Or, in some cases, to abandon those values and behave in ways they would not normally have considered. There were stories of sailors getting very drunk, or finding sweethearts halfway around the world from their wives. There were even tales of island women trading themselves for some of the white man's stock of wonderful items made of iron, like cooking pots and knives.

Was it rumors of that kind of behavior that prompted Mary to join Captain Russell on this journey?

In March, after many days of sailing in "a heavy sea," the *Emily* arrived at the South African port of Simon's Bay, to make repairs and to replace its lost boats. Mary described the town as looking like "something built for the amusement of children. . . . There is very little to interest or amuse the mind here . . ."

Whenever the *Emily* reached port, Mary sought out any European (white-skinned, English-speaking) female she might find, usually the wife of the local colonial governor. The hostess might not have realized that Mary was paying close and critical attention to everything—her home (often an elegant estate), her clothing, gardens, servants, and her manners.

By the middle of May, "we are once more embark'd on our voyage. . . . The winds continue to blow strong, the sea runs high. This I am assured is the worst part . . ." With true New England backbone, Mary went on, "I must therefore endeavor to bear it with patience, however unpleasant it is for the present." But with some pride she claimed, "I shall certainly become a good sailor at last."

Early in June, the *Emily* arrived at the remote Isle of St. Paul's, about halfway between South Africa and Australia. Shortly after sending off two boats full of sailors to catch fish, the main ship was approached by a small sloop. "It was evident from the number of men that they were Pirates. They passed close under the stern. The Capt'n called to them to keep off or he would fire into them." The pirates passed again, so close that Mary could clearly see their faces, "which bore the stamp of villains." But the sight of the *Emily's* muskets scared them off. Without even beginning a new paragraph, Mary continued, "The two boats returned loaded with some of the finest fish I ever saw. They resemble the American Shad, but fatter."

Six months after starting the journey, Mary could finally report: "June 12: The long wished for, long expected cry of 'There she blows' was heard this morning. It set every one in motion. What a bustle! The first idea it produc'd was the ship is sinking, unacquainted as I was with such scenes." Men stood on watch day and night throughout a sea voyage. The cry "There she blows!" was a welcome signal that a whale had been sighted; the water spraying up through its blowhole was usually visible first.

Instantly, everyone on board became part of a high-speed and efficient machine. When the call was heard, the crew immediately loaded the small whaleboats with sharpened harpoons and tubs of harpoon line. Once the ship was within a mile of the quarry, the small boats were launched, each carrying a mate, a boat-steerer, and four oarsmen, who would then row as hard and fast as they could. The mate egged them on with cheers and threats, always in a low voice so as not to alert the whale. Hearty competition flourished among the men, each boat tearing across the waves to be in place to throw the first harpoon.

It must have been a terrifying prospect, to face a beast whose tail alone was wider across than the boat the men were steering into position. The harpoon, connected to hundreds of feet of line, was hurled into the side of the whale, not to kill just yet, but simply to attach the boat to its prey. Now, the whale would be injured and angry. It might swim frantically for an hour or more, dragging the tiny whaleboat along behind, as it dove—called *sounding*—deep below the waves, or thrashed about in panic.

Finally, if the men were lucky, the whale would tire enough that they could row close again, this time throwing harpoons for the kill. The dead whale was towed back to the waiting ship, where the tired men still had many hours of hard work ahead of them—slicing the blubber from their prize, cooking it over fires on the ship's deck to reduce it to oil, and storing it safely in dozens of barrels in the hold. The whole ship would be slippery with oil and awash in blood, but the crew would have captured another few gallons of what, to them, was as precious as gold.

Mary gave no details about the quest on that day, only that there was no whale captured, nor would there be for many more weeks. A whaling voyage might last as long as three years, with only a few dozen days actually spent chasing and harpooning whales.

Mary wrote next about Tower Island, "so called for its peculiar shape." The shore "was strew'd with red and white coral," but "The long grass prevented my going far from the beach." She was probably wearing the long skirts and heeled boots that were currently fashionable at home—not the best clothes for exploring deserted islands. "The weather threatening rain we left this pleasant spot with regret. I believe I was the first European female that ever set foot on it."

After pausing at several ports, the *Emily* arrived at Copang Harbor, and was surrounded by several canoes full of local people wanting to trade. "Their appearance is grotesque and singular in the extreme, to one who has not been us'd to see nature in its roughest form."

That was Mary's way of informing her daughter that these men were nearly naked.

"Their dress is very simple, consisting of a strip of cloth tied round their middle." Their faces were "very open and pleasant," but "they are notorious for pilfering whatever comes in their way that is made of iron. The natives of Timor are of middling stature, of a dark copper colour, their hair straight and black . . . they have no beards and owing to this peculiarity and the smallness of their feet and hands I thought the greater part of them were women." The *Emily* traded knives for "fowls, sweet potatoes, bananas, cocoa-nuts, etc. etc."

Mary jumped at the chance to go ashore and then discovered that she was a celebrity: "Crowds of people had assembled on the beach to witness the uncommon spectacle, the sight of an English woman. As it is a place where the whale ships touch for refreshments, a white man was no novelty, but a female created a wonderful commotion." The road was lined with onlookers, as if waiting for a parade.

Following custom, the Russells were invited to visit at the home of the governor and his wife. Mary recorded the details with particular eagerness. She was surprised to find an instant friend in Madam Hazart, despite her mixed heritage: "Her father [is] a French physician, her mother a Creole of the country. She is consequently nearly white. She was carefully educated by her father, who had good sense and generosity enough to think that women have souls (quite contrary to the prevailing idea in this part of the world) . . ."

Mary must have been delighted to have been served food other than the shipboard standard of salted pork, and to have spent time in women's company after so many weeks alone with whalers.

"Towards evening visitors began to collect and we soon had the drawing room filled with all the rank and fashion that Copang could boast. Some of the ladies were very handsome and, having their faces well Chenan'd (rubbed over with slaked lime), might well pass in the evening for white women." Mary was forced by circumstance to socialize with women of color, and surprised herself by liking them!

Entertainment in the garden was "a band of music formed entirely of the governor's own slaves" playing tambourines, drums, and violins. "It was surprising to see how well they understood time. There was not a discordant sound throughout the band, composed mostly of children from seven to twelve years old."

Mary continued to visit the governor's wife nearly daily while the *Emily* was in port, and recorded a new tidbit of knowledge that must have been useful in the long months at sea with no supply of fresh milk: "They have a method here of preserving milk by boiling it down with a proposition of lump sugar. It is then made into small cakes and exposed in the sun when it hardens and will keep a long time in this state. A small piece in a cup of tea serves both purpose of sugar and cream."

When Mary expressed curiosity about some children among the servants, Madame Hazart explained that they'd been sent to her in payment of a debt, but really she had more employees than she needed already.

> Her principles and feelings would not allow her to sell human beings, but she had frequently given them to such of her friends as she was assured would use them well. . . . Madam Hazart said if I would accept one of them I might have my choice. They were three fine looking child girls, apparently about nine years old. I accordingly selected one that from her intelligent countenance I thought would answer. When we ask'd her by signs if she would go in the ship with me, appear'd highly delighted.

What Mary felt about receiving a human being as a gift, and how the arrangement worked out, we'll never know; she never mentions the child again in her diary.

When Mary said her farewell on July 31, Madame Hazart gave her a diamond ring as a parting memento, "saying, 'My dear Mrs. Russell, this ring I had made for you. It is set with my own hair. When you look at this think sometimes of your friends at Timor who will never forget you.'"

As Mary's voyage continued, the ports of call became more and more exotic, both in their names and in their offerings: "For the first time I saw the China orange in perfection, they are small but have a flavor that I think preferable to the large kind." She must have been tasting what we know as clementines, which would not have been exported as far away as Nantucket in those days.

The *Emily* was now sailing in the Far East, and "have pass'd Pulla Dama, Banda, Amboyna (where your dear Father in a former voyage had the misfortune to bury his Mate, Hezekiah Coffin, and where he only escap'd the jaws of death himself), Manippa, Ceram . . ." and later in August, "We are now steering for the Geba Passage, saw the Islands of Boo and Joey. Saw Raib Island . . . saw Pidgeon Island which is inhabited . . ."

Mary wrote of the Pacific Ocean, "The weather here is extremely variable and squally, but it is consider'd good ground for whaling."

On August 30, they "saw whales and after a toilsome chase succeeded in taking two." On September 3, "This morning early saw whales, when four boats are lower'd in pursuit. . . . The whales were so near that I could distinctly view the whole scene with a glass [meaning a telescope]. My terror was extreme . . ."

Why did Mary never describe what happened to the whales after capture? We do not hear of them getting hauled on deck or being cut up or processed into oil. There is no mention of blood or blubber or stench. Did her husband insist that she remain safely in her cabin during these scenes, to avoid the gruesome sight? Or did she not think an eyewitness report would be suitable reading for her daughter?

The *Emily* arrived at the St. David's Islands on September 17, 1823. On a previous voyage, Captain Russell had hired two natives of St. David's to help his crew during the whaling season. One, named Lorei, was the second son of the king, "but it seems his two wives, fearful that he would take another voyage, had prevented him by force from coming on board" to greet his old shipmates.

The Russells did meet with Lorei and his family when they disembarked to pay their respects to royalty:

> Your dear Father dressed the king in a white shirt and a new straw hat and presented him with knives, fish hooks, iron hoops, etc. The dress of these natives is a strip of cloth made from the rind of the cocoa-nut, but they have a frightful way of frizzing their hair which serves to protect them from the sun as well as a hat. As we were two hands short, the Capt'n agreed to take the king's third son, a fine looking lad, apparently about twenty, and another of the same age by the name of Bookalap Boohoo. . . . These people have not a warlike weapon among them, not so much as a bow and arrow. When Lorei was ask'd if they ever fought at St. Davids 'Oh, yes, plenty fight,' he said. 'But how do you fight, Lorei?' 'Oh plenty pull hair.' This was all the idea they had of war.

Nor were they as God-fearing as Mary might have wished: "They do not appear to have any religious ceremonies among them, except dancing in a ring at the full of the Moon." But they did know about taxes: "The king claims the head of every fish that is taken, as his undisputed property."

Later in September, the *Emily* encountered another ship, off the coast of New Guinea. Captain Barker of the *Nearchus* came aboard to share news. Without realizing that Mary and her husband were Americans, he had some strong words to say: "'Had you been a Yankee, Capt'n Russell, you would not have seen me on board here, for I detest and despise those Yankees!'" Mary was quite smug. "Little did he think at the moment that he was conversing with two of those detestable beings. I think when he finds it out (which he certainly will, as he has a man on board that had known your father many years) it will cause him to discard such useless prejudices for the future."

Mary was defensive when she herself became the object of "useless prejudice," but she always failed to notice her own condescending assumptions. She visited a local mosque, and was "impressed with the architecture," but faintly offended that she, as a Christian, was not welcome beyond the row of pillars and "sentries who marched to guard their sanctuary from the footstep of any other persuasion. As far as I could see of the interior, its construction was simple and extremely neat. When we turn'd to leave it, I gave a sigh for the delusion of so many thousands of my fellow beings who thus live and thus will die, ignorant of the glorious light of truth . . ."

Several days later, the *Emily* was still within sight of Papua–New Guinea, "so near that cultivated spots were very perceptible and with a good glass we could plainly perceive large villages . . . with their adjoining plantations, which show'd that the Pappua's possess'd the knowledge of agriculture however ignorant they might be in other respects . . ."

They encountered a *proa* (boat), full of natives, who threatened Mary's husband with a spear. Captain Russell quickly aimed his musket, causing the spear-holder to drop his weapon and make a *salaam*, or deep bow, of apology. The chief then came aboard wearing "a gay chintz dressing gown with a cotton handkerchief folded narrow and knotted in front, leaving the crown of his head uncovered with the hair standing up eight or ten inches. Add to this gay appearance a savage countenance, much scar'd, and you will form some idea of our guest. . . . He gazed at me and your little brother Charles with marks of astonishment. Beckoning Charles who went to him, he pass'd his hand several times over his face and then examined his light glossy hair to ascertain if it really was flesh and substance."

The next day, the *Emily* was approached by a fleet of large *proas,* rowed by men wishing to trade their exotic fruits. "After exchanging these articles for tin pots, handkerchiefs, iron hoops, etc. they took up a kind of scuttle and display'd about a dozen children of both sexes, apparently from six to twelve years, which they held up for sale. These wretched objects look'd as if nearly starv'd, and were offer'd for two fathoms of cotton cloth, which was bought in England for six-pence a yard." Mary regretted that she could not rescue "these little objects from their wretched condition, but . . . saw the children laid down again in the bottom of the boat and cover'd over with a sensation that I shall never forget as long as I live." In the very next sentence, she shifted her priority: "Inquiry was made for different kinds of vegetables which we heard they had at the time, but this was not the right season . . ."

It was the season for turtle, however. Over the next couple of weeks they were found "in abundance" along with land crabs, "which after feeding them with corn a few days, I am told are equal in flavor with a lobster."

According to Mary's account, nothing too notable happened after that:

> . . . until the 27th of November, when whales being seen, all the boats were instantly man'd and went in pursuit. It was five o'clock when the boats left the ship, the weather squally and threatening. With an anxious heart I watch'd all their motions with the glass, tho so distant were they that to the naked eye they could only be discover'd in the horizon as they rose with the swell which ran high. Directly one of the boats which prov'd to be your brother's was rapidly approaching the ship, the whale to which he was fastened running with all the strength expiring nature lent her. As they approach'd near the ship, exhausted by loss of blood, the unwieldy object slackened her pace and in a few minutes died close by the ship. By this time it was past sunset . . .

> Not until after nine o'clock did the other boats come limping home.

> . . . and how happy to see your dear Father arrive once more, owing to the roughness of the sea and anxiety of mind at being out so late. He had not a dry thread in his clothes and *this, thought I, is the way that these "sons of Ocean" earn their money that is so thoughtlessly spent at home.* Could some of the ladies whose husbands are occupied in this dangerous business have been here this few hours past, I think it would be a lesson they would not forget.

Mary imagined that anyone knowing the effort it took to keep lamps burning would be more thrifty with the oil.

Interspersed with her descriptions of islands and of whaling, Mary continued to record frequent incidents of shipboard drama:

"December 13th: [While] little Charles was amusing himself with his playthings on deck, the man at the helm seized him by the arm which had been lately broken and threw him several feet . . . with such force as nearly dislocated his shoulder. I heard him scream and ran to him . . ." The man "ran to the gangway and jumped overboard. A boat was immediately lowered and went in pursuit of him. They soon return'd with the Gentleman, who was sentenced to receive three dozen stripes for his pains. I could not plead much in his favor, for he was a most audacious character, having by his own account escap'd from a neighboring country jail in Female apparel, previous to joining the ship at Gravesend . . ."

The whaling began in earnest, and many whales were taken during the following weeks, including upon Christmas Day. A month later, Mary wrote a report off the Traitor Islands. The small boats had "put off in high glee in the pursuit" of several large whales seen at a distance. But after sunset, the boats were no longer visible from the deck of the *Emily*.

As they always carry a lantern in the boats, we hop'd as soon as it was dark to discover their lights, but in vain. . . . My terror was such that it seem'd to me I should lose my senses, but seeing the ship keeper too much frighten'd to do anything I order'd a large fire to be lit on the Cabboose and to fire guns as a direction for the boats. This I had heard spoken of as proper to be done in such cases. To my inexpressible joy about nine o'clock word was brought me that they could at intervals discover the lights heave up with the swell. They continued their torching with fresh courage and in two hours more they came alongside, bringing two whales which they had tow'd six or seven miles . . .

Mary's quick thinking had saved boatloads of tired men, as well as their prize prey.

The remainder of the letter, through January, February, and March 1824, consisted of a tally of the whale hunt, sometimes with as many as five killed in one day! There are brief entries, such as "William cut his hand" or "Tremendous weather" or, on March 5, "No land in sight, tho we are passing over the ground where the Carolines Isles are laid down in the charts. This creates anxiety." That whole week must have been wretched on board the creaking *Emily*, with comments like "squally tremendous sea," and "split the sail all to pieces."

At last, in the final entry on March 11, Mary wrote, "Looking out for Guam, towards night saw the Isle, sounded in and came to anchor off Port Aprur. 45 whales recorded to date."

There ends Mary's account. Did she mail the letter to her daughter, Mary Ann, or deliver it by hand when she next saw her?

Captain Laban Russell died in 1842 when he was sixty-two years old. Mary lived thirteen years as a widow in Rye, New York. Later on, "dear little Charles," now all grown up, disputed his mother's interpretation of his father's will and took her to court.

Mary died when she was seventy-one years old, with several grandchildren. Did she ever gather them around the fire and tell stories of her life upon the waves? Or were her moments of adventure recalled only on paper?

Mary Hayden Russell's adventure may have caused her peers to think her slightly scandalous.

   Harriet Jacobs's behavior, however, was beyond scandalous; it was illegal.

Harriet Ann Jacobs

1813–1897

"I was born a slave," wrote Harriet Ann Jacobs, in the first sentence of her memoir. *"But I never knew it till six years of happy childhood had passed away."*

Those six years gave her a taste of what life should be for every child, and became a memory to look back on during the many wretched decades to come.

‿

I f Harriet Jacobs had not learned to read and write, she would have been swallowed up in history, another faceless, nameless slave, relentlessly tormented, without anyone today knowing a single thing about her misery—or her triumph.

Being literate gave Harriet a weapon that she used to trick her pursuer once she'd escaped from bondage, and then to expose the horrors of slavery as few slaves had been able to do before, by writing a book (using the pen name Linda Brent) called *Incidents in the Life of a Slave Girl*. It is a remarkable account of her youth in the southern United States, and it is still in print more than a century after Harriet's anguished run for freedom.

Harriet and her mother, Delilah, were both "owned" by a kindly woman named Margaret Horniblow. Although it was frowned upon to teach slaves to read or write, Margaret did just that, making clever Harriet (nicknamed Hatty) an unusually educated slave child. Margaret taught Hatty how to sew, as well, a skill that would mean survival later in life.

A law against slave literacy was passed in North Carolina when Hatty was a teenager. The official wording began this way: "Whereas the teaching of slaves to read and write has a tendency to excite dissatisfaction in their minds and to produce insurrection and rebellion, to the manifest injury to the citizens of this State . . ." The law goes on to declare that it is forbidden to provide slaves with books or pamphlets, including the Bible. A white person breaking this law would be fined or imprisoned. An African American would be imprisoned or whipped, "not exceeding thirty-nine lashes nor less than twenty lashes." The same punishment of thirty-nine lashes would be given to any slave who tried to learn to read.

Harriet Jacobs was certainly "dissatisfied" and often cleverly rebellious, but knowing how to read was not the cause.

Hatty lived with her younger brother, John, and her parents, Elijah and Delilah, along with her grandmother, Molly, who worked as the cook and indispensable housekeeper at Horniblow's Tavern. Elijah was an expert carpenter, and Delilah was lucky to work indoors instead of being sent into the fields. The tavern was central to the social life in the town of Edenton, as well as the site of the county slave auctions. Young Hatty probably witnessed some of those proceedings, but they were not mentioned in her book.

When Hatty was six, her mother died. As sad as this was, she continued to live in the heart of the family who "fondly shielded" her from the reality of slavery. It took another few years and the death of her owner, Margaret Horniblow, before Hatty's life changed dramatically.

Hatty prayed that her mistress might have bestowed one final kindness: "I could not help having some hopes that she had left me free." But, "after a brief period of suspense, the will of my mistress was read, and we learned that she had bequeathed me to her sister's daughter, a child of five years old. So vanished our hopes."

Hatty wrote, "I would give much to blot out from my memory that one great wrong." Considering all that happened to her later, it is remarkable that Hatty's forgiving spirit let her remember that "while I was with her, she taught me to read and spell: and for this privilege, which so rarely falls to the lot of a slave, I bless her memory."

What Hatty would never know is that Margaret's will *had not been signed*. Hatty had been bequeathed to Margaret's little niece, Miss Mary Matilda, in a hastily scrawled addition to the will the day that Margaret died. There has since been speculation that Margaret was not the author of that fateful postscript, that perhaps the villain in Hatty's life story—Mary Matilda's father—had sneaked in to betray her.

However it happened, Hatty now learned what it meant to be a slave. She moved into the household headed by the father of her new mistress, Dr. James Norcom, called "Dr. Flint" in *Incidents in the Life of a Slave Girl*. Perhaps the instinct to remain hidden prompted Hatty's decision to disguise her characters. Along with changing her own name, Hatty gave pseudonyms to other family members, as well as to this man who would torment her all of his life.

Hatty's brother John and her Aunt Betty were both in the Norcom household, too, but the transition was still a difficult one. Not long after she arrived, "she awakened to sounds that would ring in her ears for decades: the hiss of a whip, accompanied by the pitiful pleas of a slave."

Slowly, she adjusted to her new situation, where her duties were to dress and care for "Little Miss," and to help with household chores during the child's naptime. Then came the terrible news of Hatty's father's sudden death. Hatty's owners did not allow time for mourning, as they had considered Elijah to be an untrustworthy character. "They thought he had spoiled his children, by teaching them to feel that they were human beings. This was blasphemous doctrine for a slave to teach; presumptuous in him and dangerous to the masters."

When Hatty turned fifteen, Dr. Norcom was about fifty years old, and made his intentions clear. "My master began to whisper foul words in my ear. Young as I was, I could not remain ignorant of their import." For a girl who had been raised by her grandmother to be respectful and pious, the doctor's attentions were loathsome. "He told me I was his property; that I must be subject to his will in all things."

Almost worse for Hatty was the effect that her master's behavior had on his wife, Maria. She had been only sixteen when she became the second Mrs. Norcom. She now had seven children. She was understandably hurt and angry that her husband was doggedly pursuing another woman, but she directed all her fury at Hatty, as if it were somehow her fault.

Meanwhile, Hatty had met someone—a free black man—whom she truly cared for: "I loved him with all the ardor of a young girl's first love. But when I reflected that I was a slave, and that the laws gave no sanction to the marriage of such, my heart sank within me."

A slave was not allowed to get married without permission from his or her master, which Dr. Norcom would not give. He hit her, and swore that if he caught her suitor anywhere nearby, "'I will shoot him as soon as I would a dog.'" Hatty drummed up her courage to beg Mrs. Norcom to intervene, but that woman's response was grim: "'I will have you peeled and pickled, young lady, if I ever hear you mention that subject again.'"

In the meantime, Mrs. Norcom unintentionally did Hatty a favor, insisting that Hatty no longer sleep under the same roof as her husband. She was sent back to live with Molly, her grandmother, and only work by day for the doctor's family. Hatty could finally rest at night, though Mrs. Norcom was often mean and vengeful through the working hours.

"The secrets of slavery are concealed like those of the Inquisition," Hatty revealed years later. "My master was, to my knowledge, the father of eleven slaves. But did the mothers dare to tell who was the father of their children? Did the other slaves dare to allude to it, except in whispers among themselves? No, indeed! They knew too well the terrible consequences."

When Hatty learned that her master was building a cottage outside the town, just so that he could have a secret place to take her, she knew it was time for action. What she did to protect herself may seem odd now, but her options were limited, so she relied on cleverness and courage. Rather than become an unwilling victim of Dr. Norcom's lust, she started a relationship with another white man in town, Sam Sawyer. He was a friend of her family who would be kind, and possibly even help her to freedom. Hatty did not confide in her grandmother, knowing the old woman would find this choice difficult to accept, but her secrecy ended when she became pregnant.

Hatty had been hoping that Dr. Norcom might be angry enough to sell her when he heard the news, allowing her new beau a chance to be the buyer, but she had underestimated his determination. The law stated that as long as a mother was enslaved, any child born to her was a slave as well. The doctor soon had a new, baby boy slave, named Joseph, after Hatty's uncle. The only good outcome was that Hatty, mother of a new-born, had a little time before the harassment was renewed.

For those slaves not willing to succumb to abuse and humiliation, there were only two possibilities: to fight back, or to run away. Fighting back took many shapes. Hatty tried to outsmart her master. Others decided that only violent action could change anything.

When Hatty was a teenager, a slave named Nat Turner, in the neighboring state of Virginia, led an uprising that resulted in the deaths of fifty-five white people. Patrols, or "musters," were established—groups of white men acting as an unofficial police force, to watch, follow, search, and plunder the homes of African Americans. One of the things they were looking for was books or printed paper of any kind.

Hatty learned that her grandmother's house would be searched by the patrols. She knew that "nothing annoyed them so much as to see colored people living in comfort and respectability." Deviously, she worked all day to make the house clean and lovely. "I arranged every thing in my grandmother's house as neatly as possible. I put white quilts on the beds, and decorated some of the rooms with flowers." Perhaps the flowers irked the patrolmen, but the discovery of books and papers led to Hatty being roughly questioned.

When Hatty was nineteen years old, she informed Dr. Norcom that she was pregnant for the second time.

"He rushed from the house, and returned with a pair of shears. I had a fine head of hair; and he often railed about my pride of arranging it nicely. He cut every hair close to my head, storming and swearing all the time."

Despite the protection offered by the baby's father, Sam, the doctor kept his anger burning throughout the pregnancy, even hitting Hatty, and often hurling verbal abuse.

"When they told me my new-born babe was a girl, my heart was heavier than it had ever been before. Slavery is terrible for men, but it is far more terrible for women."

Hatty had just delivered baby Louisa into Doctor Norcom's official possession. She was permitted to live with the baby for two years at her grandmother's house before the doctor offered Hatty a choice: become his mistress and live in comfort, or be banished to his son's plantation. "Junior" was preparing his estate to welcome his new bride after their upcoming wedding, so Hatty's labors would be heavy. Much to the doctor's irritation, she chose the plantation, leaving her children behind. "I had many sad thoughts as the old wagon jolted on."

Hatty now toiled by day and took what was known as a "slave's holiday" at night—walking six miles across unlit fields to see her family for a few precious minutes before walking back in the dark to her quarters. This routine came to an abrupt end when she heard that her children were to arrive on the plantation the next day "to be broke in," meaning that the doctor's new plan was to make Hatty watch, helplessly, while her children suffered as field workers.

That night, Hatty was stirred to serious action: "At half past twelve I stole softly down stairs. I stopped on the second floor, thinking I heard a noise. I felt my way down into the parlor, and looked out of the window. The night was so intensely dark that I could see nothing. I raised the window very softly and jumped out. Large drops of rain were falling, and the darkness bewildered me. I dropped on my knees, and breathed a short prayer to God for guidance and protection . . ."

She went first to say good-bye to her grandmother and to kiss the sleeping Joseph and Louisa. "I feared the sight of my children would be too much for my full heart; but I could not go into the uncertain future without one last look . . ."

In fact, she would kiss her children only once again during the next many years.

In her book, Hatty did not name the friend who bravely sheltered her for the next few days, but one night, she wrote, "my pursuers came into such close vicinity that I concluded they had tracked me to my

$100 REWARD

WILL be given for the apprehension and delivery of my Servant Girl HARRIET. She is a light mulatto, 21 years of age, about 5 feet 4 inches high, of a thick and corpulent habit, having on her head a thick covering of black hair that curls naturally, but which can be easily combed straight. She speaks easily and fluently, and has an agreeable carriage and address. Being a good seamstress, she has been accustomed to dress well, has a variety of very fine clothes, made in the prevailing fashion, and will probably appear, if abroad, tricked out in gay and fashionable finery. As this girl absconded from the plantation of my son without any known cause or provocation, it is probable she designs to transport herself to the North.

The above reward, with all reasonable charges, will be given for apprehending her, or securing her in any prison or jail within the U. States.

All persons are hereby forewarned against harboring or entertaining her, or being in any way instrumental in her escape, under the most rigorous penalties of the law.

JAMES NORCOM.

Edenton, N. C. June 30

hiding-place." She flew into a thicket of bushes behind the house. Crouching there, she was bitten by a poisonous snake and barely staggered back to safety. Her friend applied a poultice of warm ashes and vinegar, which relieved the pain somewhat, but Hatty knew a better hiding spot was needed.

"The search for me was kept up with more perseverance than I had anticipated." Doctor Norcom posted notices all over the country, offering a reward in return for Hatty's capture.

Help appeared as if in answer to Hatty's prayers. The kind wife of a local slave-owner asked Hatty's grandmother if she could help, on condition that she never be named. Molly apparently trusted and confided in her. Hatty later wrote, "I received a message to leave my friend's house at such an hour, and go to a certain place where a friend would be waiting for me. As a matter of prudence no names were mentioned. I had no means of conjecturing who I was to meet, or where I was going . . ."

Hatty's destination was the woman's spare bedroom, which was used for storage and kept locked. Only the mistress and cook knew she was there. But Dr. Norcom was furiously seeking revenge. It was in his power to imprison Hatty's family in order to force them to tell where she had gone. Hatty's son, Joseph, and little daughter, Louisa, watched over by their Uncle John and an old aunt, were all placed in the town jail. The doctor rightly guessed that Hatty would be tempted to risk her own safety to visit them in secret. But she got a note from her brother pleading with her to remain hidden: "'Wherever you are, dear sister, I beg you not to come here. We are all much better off than you are. If you come, you will ruin us all . . .'" Hatty forced herself to trust that her brother and aunt would care for the children.

She soon had another fright. The doctor's voice echoed through the house where she was concealed in an upstairs room. Dr. Norcom was rushing off to New York City because he'd heard a rumor that Hatty had been seen there, but first he was asking to borrow five hundred dollars from the very woman who was hiding Hatty!

Norcom's trip was a failure, of course, and he returned in debt. He received an offer from a slave trader, unaware that the man had been hired by Sam Sawyer, the father of Joseph and Louisa. The trader proposed to pay Dr. Norcom $900 for Hatty's brother, and $800 more for her two children. The doctor needed money and made the sale, making Hatty as happy a woman as a fugitive slave could be: "The darkest cloud that hung over my life had rolled away. Whatever slavery might do to me, it could not shackle my children." The trader honored his agreement to deliver Joseph and Louisa back into Molly's loving care, much to Dr. Norcom's angry frustration.

As it turned out, many years would go by before Hatty's optimistic hope of truly free children became a reality. For now, however, their safety gave Hatty strength when she was spotted by a curious servant and forced to move quickly out of the refuge of the spare bedroom. Arrangements were made for her to hide on a boat overnight. "Betty," a friend and fellow slave, brought her a disguise—the jacket, trousers, and hat of a sailor—and then coached her. "'Put your hands in your pockets and walk rickety, like de sailors,'" she said.

Walking "rickety" was not difficult; her weeks of inactivity, combined with fear, must have made Hatty's legs feel pretty shaky on her way to the wharf.

"I was to remain on board till near dawn, and then they would hide me in Snaky Swamp till my uncle Phillip has prepared a place of concealment for me." Ever since being bitten, Hatty was horrified by snakes. For the following week, she hid on the boat each night but spent her days in the swamp with her loyal friend, "Pete." "I saw snake after snake crawling around us. . . . But even those large, venomous snakes were less dreadful in my imagination than the white men in that community called civilized."

When her new hiding spot was ready, she blackened her face with charcoal and dressed again in the sailor disguise. Walking through town, she passed close by her old sweetheart, Sam Sawyer, but he did not recognize her.

"'You must make the most of this walk,' said my friend, Peter, 'for you may not have another very soon.'" It would be nearly seven years before she walked that street again.

What Hatty's uncle had set up for her was a crawl space over her grandmother's storage shed, above the room and under the roof. It was nine feet long, seven feet wide, and little more than three feet high at its peak, with a steeply sloping ceiling. Between her and the sky were shingles; between her and the storeroom below was a mat on a rough board floor, a trapdoor, and a million tiny red insects. It was utterly dark inside, day and night. Her uncle had left behind a gimlet, a small hand tool for boring holes through wood. When she guessed from sounds that it was evening, Hatty patiently and repeatedly drilled through her wall until she had made a hole one inch across. This was her tiny window for light, air, and occasional glimpses of her precious children.

In Hatty's book, *Incidents in the Life of a Slave Girl*, seven years pass by in fewer than fifty pages. But, "O, those long gloomy days with no object for my eye to rest upon and no thoughts to occupy my mind, except the dreary past and the uncertain future!"

Hatty's grandmother kept her fed with both food and news: the ongoing chase, family gossip, and the preparations for Christmas. Molly brought Hatty material so that she could sew clothes and toys for the children by the beam of her tiny window. During the winters, it got icy-cold in the attic. Hatty recalled that her "limbs were benumbed by inaction, and the cold filled them with cramp. I had a very painful sensation of coldness in my head; even my face and tongue stiffened, and I lost the power of speech."

As the months and then the years passed by, Hatty watched and listened to her children growing up. Although they missed their mother, their grandmother tended them with close attention, while the lives of the surrounding adults were slowly unfolding.

Dr. Norcom went again to New York to look for Hatty. Sam Sawyer ran for Congress and won. Despite his promise, made years ago, Sam still had not freed his children. Although it may now seem odd that a white father would officially possess his own darker-skinned children, it was acceptable in that time and place. As a congressman, Sam made plans to leave North Carolina, taking Hatty's brother, John, as his personal slave. Hatty knew Sam would stop by her grandmother's house to say good-bye and to leave instructions regarding Joseph and Louisa. This rare opportunity to meet him compelled her to take a huge risk.

As Hatty tells it in her book, she crept down through the trap door, her weakened ankles barely supporting her. She hid behind a flour barrel until she had a chance to speak to him. He was shocked to see her there, but renewed his vow to liberate their children. He told her he'd do his best to purchase her, as well.

Hatty was now inspired to use writing as a tool in building the life she dreamed of. She again climbed down from her attic, this time to meet with her old friend "Pete," to convince him to help in her plan. She wrote a letter to Dr. Norcom, from a made-up address in the North, pretending not to know that he'd already sold her children, and asking to buy them. "Pete" was to arrange to have the letter mailed from somewhere in New York, using a "trusty seaman" as the postman. She enclosed a misleading note to her grandmother in the same envelope, knowing that the doctor would read it.

As Hatty anticipated, her furious master slammed through Molly's door just a few days later. Hatty positioned herself to listen to the outcome of her maneuvers. But, instead of reading what she'd written, the doctor substituted a phony letter claiming that Hatty was ashamed of running away and was asking her grandmother if she could come home. Dr. Norcom tried to trick Molly into encouraging Hatty's return this way.

This was a turning point for Hatty. As a present-day biographer put it, "She no longer felt herself Norcom's victim, but his enemy." Being his enemy meant that she felt she could fight back. Her writing had given her a power she'd never had before. She started a campaign to enrage and confuse the doctor, having a steady stream of letters sent from as far away as Canada.

Hatty also began to climb down often into the storeroom, to exercise and strengthen her legs. She was going to need them for what she had in mind.

Meanwhile, her brother John had escaped while serving Sam Sawyer in New York. Sam had a new wife, a white woman named Lavinia, and a new baby, Laura. Hatty's next worry came when Lavinia met Hatty's children and wished to adopt them!

Hatty jumped on an offer to send Louisa north to see Sam's family instead, hoping the child would have brighter prospects. The night before her daughter left, Hatty sneaked into Louisa's room, to introduce herself and to spend the last few hours together. She swore the girl to secrecy as they shared a memorable reunion before parting, "with such feelings as only a slave mother can experience." Not long after Louisa's departure, Hatty heard that her daughter had been "given" as a gift to Sam's cousin. Once again, Sam had failed to free his children.

In January of 1842, Hatty's cousin, called "Fanny" in her narrative, was sold to a local man. Her four daughters were auctioned off to the master of a distant estate. "Fanny" was devastated, and ran away, but found concealment close by Molly's house on King Street. Hatty had a fellow fugitive, even if she couldn't see her. Throughout all the ups and downs in Hatty's life, she remained huddled in her gloomy crawl space, fervently envisioning and patiently praying for an opportunity to change her circumstances. Finally, "the faithful friend who had helped her survive in the swamp appeared at Molly's door with word of a ship that could prove a means of escape to free soil."

Despite the heartbreak of leaving her son, and as unnerving as this must have felt, Hatty was determined to seize the chance. But then word came of a captured runaway slave who had died painfully after a vicious whipping. This tragic news so distressed her grandmother that Hatty faltered. She allowed her cousin, "Fanny," using the agreed-upon false name of "Linda," to be a substitute in her place on the ship northward.

Rain and rough water kept the boat in the harbor for three extra days. Was it good luck or bad luck that Molly forgot to lock the door of her house while Hatty was downstairs with her? They were disturbed, and Hatty was sighted. Molly immediately changed her mind and urged her beloved granddaughter to leave on the boat, knowing that she'd likely never see her again.

Hatty spent the evening hours with her son. They had not spoken to each other in seven years, but he swore that he knew she'd been there, and often misled her pursuers on purpose. Together with Molly, they knelt for a final prayer before Hatty said farewell.

Even when writing her memoirs ten years later, Hatty avoided giving any details of her escape. But she wrote that after lying down for most of seven years, "I never could tell how we reached the wharf. My brain was all of a whirl, and my limbs tottered under me."

Once on the boat, Hatty was taken to a cabin where she found her cousin. The kind captain was confused, now having two "Linda"s in hiding. He had to warn them to hush the noise of their delighted reunion.

Hatty vividly remembered her first morning on board: "O, the beautiful sunshine! The exhilarating breeze! And I could enjoy them without fear or restraint. I had never realized what grand things air and sunlight are till I had been deprived of them."

Having "Fanny" aboard with her meant that they could share the joy, as well as the anxiety, of facing a world often imagined but without any grasp of its reality.

When the boat arrived in Philadelphia, "Fanny" and Hatty took their first steps as free women, and Hatty set out on her very first shopping trip. "I found the shops and bought some double veils and gloves for Fanny and myself." She did not understand the money, or the price the shopkeeper named. Not wanting to appear obviously a stranger, she offered a gold coin and then counted her change to calculate the value of the items she had purchased.

Hatty and "Fanny" were greeted by a black man, the Reverend Jeremiah Durham, who was a representative of the General Vigilance Committee in Philadelphia. He, and particularly his wife, provided a warm and informative welcome to the free world. Hatty stayed with the Durhams in their little house on Barley Street, slowly absorbing new sights and ideas. "One day she took me to an artist's room and showed me the portraits of some of her children. I had never seen any paintings of colored people before, and they seemed to be beautiful."

After a few days, Hatty continued to New York City, where she found her own beautiful daughter, seemingly once more betrayed by Sam Sawyer. Louisa, now nine, had not been sent to school as promised and was working as a waiting-maid.

Hatty's dream was to have a little home where she might be with her children after so many years apart. But first she needed to get a job and earn a living—without having to provide a reference from a former employer. She was eventually hired by Mrs. Willis, as a nurse for her new baby. It seemed that Hatty should now be more settled, but the next several years were full of drama, including the arrival of her son from Edenton, the death of Mrs. Willis and remarriage of Mr. Willis, a year of living abroad in London, England, and continued efforts on the part of Dr. Norcom to reclaim his valuable "possession."

In 1850, eight years after Hatty's flight from Edenton, there came another setback for escaped slaves living in New York and elsewhere in the North. A new law, called the Fugitive Slave Act, proclaimed that if a runaway were discovered, even in a state that did not permit slavery, that slave could be dragged back to his or her owner and punished as the owner saw fit. This law reintroduced fear into every minute of Hatty's day. "I was, in fact, a slave in New York, as subject to slave laws as I had been in a Slave State. Strange incongruity in a State called free!"

Finally news came that Hatty had longed to hear. Dr. Norcom had died. "I cannot say, with truth, that the news of my old master's death softened my feelings towards him. There are wrongs which even the grave does not bury."

Respite from his pursuit was short-lived. Norcom's daughter still considered Hatty desirable property. According to Mrs. Horniblow's questionable will, Mary Matilda and her husband, Daniel Messmore (called "Mr. Dodge" in the book), were Hatty's actual "owners." They were now estranged from the Norcom family and in desperate need of money. They wrote to Hatty, smoothly asking that she either return to work for them or pay them to purchase herself.

In those days, every visitor to the city was announced in the newspaper. Hatty scrutinized the daily listings for the name she feared. One morning she came into the kitchen just as the servant boy was lighting the fire, using the newspaper as kindling. Hatty snatched the paper away from the flame, and yes, that was the day when the dreaded arrival was announced.

Hatty's employer, the second Mrs. Willis, told Hatty to take her baby, Lilian, with her into hiding, knowing that the pursuers would be forced to return the baby to its mother should Hatty be captured. This would provide a little more time to find a solution. After a couple of anxious days, Hatty received a note from Mrs. Willis telling thunderous news in just a few words: "I am rejoiced to tell you that the money for your freedom has been paid to Mr. Dodge. Come home tomorrow. I long to see you and my sweet babe."

Hatty was torn between profound gratitude and disgust. "My brain reeled as I read these lines. A gentleman near me said, 'It's true; I have seen the bill of sale.' *The bill of sale!* Those words struck me like a blow. So I was sold at last! A human being sold in the free city of New York!"

When Hatty wrote her book in 1852, she did something that no one before her had had the courage to do; she discussed quite honestly how young enslaved women were repeatedly mistreated. "If God has bestowed beauty upon her, it will prove her greatest curse. That which commands admiration in the white woman only hastens the degradation of the female slave."

Hatty resisted writing her history until after she turned forty. Her anger burst through onto the page, aimed at Americans in the northern states who she felt had ignored the plight of slaves for decades. "Why are ye silent, ye free men and women of the north? Why do your tongues falter in the maintenance of the right? Would that I had more ability! But my heart is so full and my pen is so weak!"

Hatty ended her book with the chapter about her liberation, but she lived until she was eighty-four years old. The world around her underwent many profound changes during her lifetime. She was alive to witness the Civil War, where slavery was a central issue in the conflict between the northern, "free" Union states and the southern, slave-holding Confederate states. And she was alive to greet Abraham Lincoln's significant proclamation that would end slavery in the United States of America.

Hatty worked tirelessly throughout the war and for the rest of her life, helping refugees, organizing medical care for freed slaves, raising money to build an orphanage, and teaching. She continued to come up against white people with prejudice, as she would still if she were alive today. But her trials had taught her that "I can testify, from my own experience and observations, that slavery is a curse to the whites as well as to the blacks."

Perhaps most importantly, Hatty and her daughter together founded a school called the Jacobs Free School, where she could be certain that African-American children would learn to read and to write.

Harriet Jacobs watched her children, and seven passing years, through a tiny peephole. Although her view was constricted, her writing addressed the enormous issues of freedom and truth. And her vision of heaven was a small, tidy home where she could live with her children.

Meanwhile, in England, Isabella Beeton staged a quiet revolution of her own. She believed that women who created an orderly home for their families were providing unequaled leadership and nurturing. Her writing changed the domestic world forever.

Isabella Beeton and Harriet Jacobs each published her book in the same year, 1861.

Isabella Beeton

1836–1865

What moved me, in the first instance, to attempt a work like this, was the discomfort and suffering which I had seen brought upon men and women by household mismanagement. I have always thought that there is no more fruitful source of family discontent than a housewife's badly-cooked dinners and untidy ways.

ے

Mrs. Beeton's Book of Household Management *was one of the most popular books in England the year it was published, probably because nothing like it had ever been issued before.* Among many other things, the book told how many larks were needed for a Lark Pie (nine), how to tell the difference between an epileptic seizure and a fit brought on by drunkenness or opium poisoning, what to remember when "Going out with the carriage," how to make curds and whey, how to cook a swan, provided three and half pages of "General Remarks on Eggs," outlined the medicinal uses of asparagus, told how to conduct an agreeable conversation ("small disappointments, petty annoyances, and other every-day incidents, should never be mentioned to your friends"), gave a reminder of the "Extreme Timidity of the Hare," instructed how to dust (using either "a brush made of long feathers, or a goose's wing"), how to care for horses and stables, how to understand real estate law, what to use if you have no cream for your tea ("1 new-laid egg"), what to do if you swallow arsenic, how to write a will, what time your cook should rise in the morning, the history of chocolate ... The list is endless. Or rather, the list is 1,112 pages and 2,751 items long.

The book provided the answers to any question that might ever be asked about running a home and family. That may not sound like exciting material for a best-seller, but many readers were convinced that having a copy of Mrs. Beeton's book would guarantee a peaceful marriage and a contented life. One of the reasons for its success was that it was the first time that anyone had written down cooking recipes in the sensible format that is still used today, or collected so much useful information in one place.

Isabella Mayson—or Bella, as she liked to be called—had married Samuel Beeton when she was twenty years old, and began writing the book a year later. How did such a young woman have the experience to create *Mrs. Beeton's Book of Household Management?* Well, she has been accused of stealing many of the recipes in the book from more experienced chefs. But she also had lots of practice growing up—she was the eldest of twenty-one brothers and sisters!

Bella Mayson's father died when she was four years old and big sister to three younger siblings. Bella's mother, Elizabeth, knew that her only chance at making a home for her children was finding someone else to marry. She wrote to an old friend, Henry Dorling, whose own wife had recently died, leaving four children in his care. Elizabeth needed a man with a steady job. Henry needed a woman to look after his motherless brood. It was the perfect match for each of them, apart from the question of where they would settle. Both Henry's house and Elizabeth's home on Milk Street were deemed too small for the double-sized family, which also included Elizabeth's mother, called Granny Jerram.

The solution was unique.

Henry worked as Clerk of the Course at the Epsom racetrack, a job that carried much prestige and responsibility. He was in charge of organizing the horse races at this fashionable course, from scheduling and track conditions to the intake of money. Instead of buying a regular house, Henry moved everyone into the splendid new Grand Stand at the racetrack, where "there was an immense, pillared hall, a great stone staircase, a thirty-yard-long saloon, four refreshment rooms, and a warren of committee and retiring rooms." This became the nursery for the ever-growing number of children, as Elizabeth and Henry eventually added another thirteen to their original eight. They slept on cots in the offices, easily put away when the general public arrived for race days. The Grand Stand kitchen was well equipped to cook for three thousand race-goers and stocked with dishes enough to serve them. Imagine taking a turn on kitchen duty in the days before automatic dishwashers!

During Derby week, when the Grand Stand was bustling with paying race-goers, the children were sent off in groups of two or three to spend a few days with various relatives, or to Henry's other office in town. Bella later referred to the chore of moving "that living cargo of children," along with the clothing and playthings that went with them.

There is no mention of Bella's education (she was probably too busy babysitting!) until she was sixteen. After briefly attending a school in Islington, her generous stepfather arranged for her to study in Germany, where young ladies (not only gentlemen) could receive a fine education. There she learned to play the piano beautifully and to speak German and French. Bella also had her first proper training in a kitchen, and was commended by the headmistress for her flair in the culinary arts.

At Miss Heidel's School in Germany, Bella Mayson re-encountered her childhood friends, the Beeton sisters. On her return to England, it was natural that she should meet with their charming brother, Samuel, as well.

Sam's shining professional moment had come the previous year when he became the first British publisher of a hugely popular American book called *Uncle Tom's Cabin,* by Harriet Beecher Stowe. This book told the stories, the sorrows, and quiet triumphs of several slaves in the southern United States. It sold 200,000 copies in Britain in its first year.

But Sam was even keener about the magazines he published, always coming up with new ideas for content, and for selling more copies. Unfortunately, Sam's head for business was not as sharp as his eye for innovative material. He couldn't seem to keep hold of the profits from his projects. This is where Bella hoped she could help. Although gentlewomen were not encouraged to work in the mid-1800s, or to pursue any sort of interest beyond the hobby level, being able to keep accounts and understand numbers was considered a feminine quality. After all, who else would manage the household budget and pay the servants and the merchants' bills? Men were off earning the money; women needed to learn how to spend it wisely.

Bella's stepfather, Henry, did not like Sam too well, but for some reason he agreed to their engagement. The custom of courtship in those days consisted of the man visiting the woman on Sunday afternoons in the company of her family. They might occasionally go to a concert or play, accompanied by a chaperon. Time alone was almost impossible.

After about six months of critical scrutiny, Sam nearly gave up, and stopped coming to the house for a while. This may have been frustrating for the engaged couple, but it was lucky for history, because it meant that they wrote letters often. Bella asked her fiancé to burn her letters, but he kept most of them for the rest of his life—nearly forty were found in one of his pockets when he died.

Although dependent on horses, mail service was much quicker in those days than it is now, and a letter posted in the morning might be delivered the same afternoon. Bella wrote more often than Sam did, so it sometimes felt like a lopsided conversation. She frequently pushed Sam to visit her, but then regretted her outburst in the next letter. Mostly she was eager, longing, for her married life to begin. "We shall get on as merrily as crickets," she told Sam. It is easy to track the growth of attachment between the young sweethearts by looking at the signatures. From the early, almost formal "Yours most affection-ately, Isabella Mayson," the warmth increases to "Yours with all love's devotion, Bella Mayson."

Sam and Bella's wedding, in 1856, took place at the Grand Stand in Epsom, with eight bridesmaids and plenty of champagne. Bella's dress was made of white satin. Her stepfather's wedding gift of a white piano was clearly intended for Bella, but of course Sam loved to hear her play.

Several months after her honeymoon in Europe, and already preg-nant, Bella began to write articles about cookery and fashion for one of her husband's publications, called *The Englishwoman's Domestic Magazine: An Illustrated Journal Combining Practical Information, Instruction, and Amusement.* Bella's lifelong concern with spending money wisely was evident in her first appearance in print. She addressed her readers directly, urging them to buy their supplies in bulk:

> To wives and housekeepers
> . . . the purchase of an ounce of this thing, or a quarter of a pound of that, is an error. . . . potatoes should come in a sack . . . apples by the bushel . . . you will, upon the whole, have more and pay less; be free of the worry of sending out continually for small supplies, and have at hand a stock to meet emergencies.

In the spring of 1857, Bella began a regular column, one month after her twenty-first birthday and just before the birth of her first son, named Samuel for his father. But the baby was not healthy, and died of croup when he was only three months old. Babies were far more likely to die in those days, without the medicines that are now available. Few families were lucky enough not to lose at least one infant.

Bella missed writing one month's column, but she got straight back to work, despite the sadness she must have been feeling. She became more involved in the fashion pages of the *Englishwoman's Domestic Magazine,* encouraging her readers to think more about their clothing and style—an interest that only the wealthy and unoccupied women of society had followed until then.

Bella made dress and embroidery patterns available for order by the magazine-reading public, something that had not been done before. Her knowledge of French helped make Parisian fashions more accessible to the English readership. She also seems to have translated French culinary instructions, and perhaps French novels for use as serialized fiction. Printing books a chapter at a time in a monthly magazine was a well-established ploy to entice readers back for more.

As Bella juggled her new duties as a wife and homemaker along with work, she realized that all young brides must find themselves jarred by the sudden expectation that they should know all the things their mothers had learned in a lifetime of experience.

During this time in England, a new social class was emerging: between the well-bred upper class and the struggling working class, there was now a middle class. Traditionally, only those born into nobility could enjoy a privileged life, but now there were merchants and businessmen, attorneys and bankers, who were financially successful and who owned homes—often more than one. At the same time, swarms of young people moving from the country to the big city of London were available for hire. In many cases, the only thing a country girl knew how to do was to help keep a house. That's what she'd been doing on a farm or in her own home in the village, after all. She could be employed in exchange for a place to sleep and her meals. Even people in the middle class could afford servants.

Usually, the household was considered a woman's realm. Men were expected to earn the money, and their wives were expected to spend it on making the home an appealing place to come back to after a hard day of business or politics. Men did not give much thought to the astounding range of skills required to run a house well. There was no training for young wives beyond what they may have learned from their mothers. They were often dependent on the experience of the servants.

Probably the most important servant was the cook. In Isabella's words, "It is upon her that the whole responsibility of the business of the kitchen rests." Providing four meals a day (breakfast, dinner or luncheon, tea, and supper) for the family and the staff was an enormous undertaking. When guests came to dine, or to visit for several days, the task was multiplied.

In Isabella's day, most households were not equipped with electricity. There were no refrigerators, no microwaves, no toasters, no blenders, no electric can openers—no cans! (Cans, called "tins" in England, were first made of heavy iron. They were invented for use by the British Navy in 1813, and they came with the instruction: "Cut round the top near the outer edge with a chisel and hammer.") The fuel used for cooking was coal or wood, and the rooms were lit with gaslight. The heat and smells from the ovens and burning gas could be nearly overwhelming.

To help new housewives, Bella and Sam introduced another feature to the monthly *Englishwoman's Domestic Magazine,* something beyond fashion forecasts, natural history lessons, and the fancy colored illustrations. They created what was called a "supplement" that could be purchased for three pence more—an extra manual with recipes, serving advice, and tips on keeping a home running smoothly.

Bella's idea of putting two years' worth of supplements together into one volume seemed at first to be a simple way of creating a cookbook. Most of the writing had been done already; all that was needed was some organization and filling in here and there. But, in her introduction, Bella confessed that it was a task far bigger than she'd anticipated: "I must frankly own, that if I had known, beforehand, that this book would have cost me the labour which it has, I should never have been courageous enough to commence it."

That may be the summation of most writers' feelings when partway through a new endeavor, but Bella's book turned out to be FIVE HUNDRED AND FIFTY-SIX THOUSAND WORDS!! (As a comparison, the book you are reading is less than one-tenth that length.) Even the full title was a mouthful: *The Book of Household Management: Comprising information for the Mistress, Housekeeper, Cook, Kitchen-Maid, Butler, Footman,*

Coachman, Valet, Upper and Under House-Maids, Lady's-Maid, Maid-of-all-Work, Laundry-Maid, Nurse and Nurse-Maid, Monthly Wet and Sick Nurses, etc. etc. Also Sanitary, Medical, & Legal Memoranda: with a History of the Origin, Properties, and Uses of all Things Connected with Home Life and Comfort.

Bella's intention was to make ordinary women knowledgeable, skilled, and efficient, by providing information that would allow them not to fumble. "Dine we must," she wrote, "and we may as well dine elegantly as well as wholesomely." The book began with these words: "AS WITH THE COMMANDER OF AN ARMY, or the leader of any enterprise, so is it with the mistress of a house." And Bella went on—for more than 2,500 pages—to illuminate quite a stunning range of essential wisdom. In the process, she did several things that no one else had done before. She listed the recipes in alphabetical order, and she introduced what were thought of as "foreign" foods to the English housewife; recipes for Dampfnudeln (German puddings), or curried beef, or Spanish bread had not been commonly available before. ("The bread in the south of Spain is delicious: it is white as snow, close as cake, and yet very light; the flavour is most admirable, for the wheat is good and pure, and the bread well kneaded.")

Following the tradition of the *Englishwomen's Domestic Magazine,* where botany was part of gardening articles and chemistry might come under cooking or nursing, Bella provided an extensive history for many of the ingredients of her recipes. From cloves and Egyptian geese, to melons and herring, she shared fascinating details on where food came from.

Perhaps the most lasting contribution to future generations of culinary artists was twofold: she standardized both the measurements and the format of recipes. Until then, directions might have included using "a pinch" of this or "a handful" of that. Bella introduced the teaspoon, the tablespoon, and the cup, explaining the exact amount that was meant by those terms.

She also popularized a layout that all recipes would follow, beginning the instructions with a list of the ingredients. As obvious as this seems today, it was not then the custom—often an ingredient would be mentioned when its time came to enter the recipe, much as a new character could suddenly make an entrance in a story. A woman named Eliza Acton, who wrote a cookbook a few years earlier than Bella, had been the first to use this model, but Bella often gets the credit, and certainly she perfected the system. Having a complete list of ingredients available at a glance made things simpler, and Bella then made "a plain statement of the mode of preparing each dish, and a careful estimate of its cost, the number of people for whom it is sufficient, and the time when it is seasonable."

Here is an example, in her recipe for Honey Cake:

1758. **INGREDIENTS**—½ breakfast-cupful of sugar, 1 breakfast-cupful of rich sour cream, 2 breakfast-cupfuls of flour, ½ teaspoonful of carbonate of soda, honey to taste.

Mode.—Mix the sugar and cream together; dredge in the flour, with as much honey as will flavour the mixture nicely; stir it well, that all the ingredients may be thoroughly mixed; add the carbonate of soda, and beat the cake well for another 5 minutes; put it into a buttered tin, bake it from ½ to ¾ hour, and let it be eaten warm.

Time. ½ to ¾ hour.

Average cost. 8d.

Sufficient for 3 or 4 persons.

Seasonable at any time.

Some of the other desserts and sweets have delicious-sounding names, like "Dutch Flummery," "Fairy Butter," "Roly-Poly Jam Pudding," or "A Nice Plain Cake for Children."

Bella's recommendations for baby food, however, are not so appealing: "Baked flour, when cooked into a pale brown mass, and finely powdered, makes a far superior food to the others, and may be considered as a very useful diet." Bella also quotes Florence Nightingale, the renowned nurse, on the subject of the best diet for children: "Let them eat meat and drink milk, or half a glass of light beer . . ."

Bella offered dozens of food categories, such as Vegetables, Fishes, Common Hog, Puddings and Pastry, Quadrupeds (animals with four legs), and Invalid cookery (for people who are ill). Under Invalid Cookery, for instance, there is a variety of offerings to tempt the appetite of a sick person, including Barley Gruel, Baked Beef Tea, Stewed Calf's Foot, Nutritious Coffee, Eel Broth, Egg Wine, and Toast Sandwiches:

INGREDIENTS: Thin cold toast, thin slices of bread-and-butter, pepper and salt to taste.
Mode: Place a very thin piece of cold toast between 2 slices of thin bread-and-butter in the form of a sandwich, adding a seasoning of pepper and salt.

She also gave useful advice on selecting the best rabbit: "For boiling, choose rabbits with smooth and sharp claws, as that denotes they are young: should these be blunt and rugged, the ears dry and tough, the animal is old." And how to serve it after cooking: "Dish it, and smother it either with onion, mushroom, or liver sauce, or parsley-and-butter . . ."

The original cover of *The Book of Household Management* clearly states "*Edited By* Mrs. Isabella Beeton," a firm declaration that all the information within had not necessarily originated from her pen, but that she had collected, modified, and refined the recipes and other advice. Although she has been accused of plagiarism and using other people's work, there were precedents for this kind of literary assemblage. The Brothers Grimm, for instance, had used a similar technique when gathering the fairy stories and folklore identified as *Grimm's Fairy Tales;* they spoke to dozens of women and raked up old family legends and classic yarns before choosing which versions to copy down for posterity.

When Bella lifted a recipe from the book of a famous and reputable chef, she usually trusted that it worked and did not test it in her own kitchen. However, there were dozens of foods that she *did* test and perhaps alter, adding to the hours of labor that went into the original version of the book.

In some cases, Bella gave credit to the chefs she was "borrowing" from, but not always. Eliza Acton, in particular, felt that credit to her was neglected. Occasionally (without naming), Bella acknowledged the existence of another cook in the text, as in this line: "A great authority in culinary matters suggests the addition of a little cayenne pepper in gingerbread. Whether it be advisable to use this latter ingredient or not, we leave our readers to decide."

If she wasn't busy enough during the winter of 1858, Bella became pregnant again, but found time to open a soup kitchen for the village children, testing a recipe, *Useful Soup for Benevolent Purposes*, that she later put in her book.

The Beetons' second baby was born just as Bella finished the testing and main editing on the *Book of Household Management*. Following common custom, he was also named Samuel. By this time, the Beetons were living in a village on the outskirts of London, but Bella worked alongside her husband in a newly acquired city office. She caused quite a flurry of upset on the morning train when she joined the ranks of male commuters.

The baby was six months old when his parents took a business trip to Paris without him. Although far too busy in her normal life to write a journal, Bella kept notes of the excursion in a miniature leather diary. She wrote with a pencil in the tiny squares, keeping track of the dates, the places, and the cost of everything, as well as brief character sketches of their fellow travelers. "Square face," she wrote, or "sleek Doctor with a white beard and moustaches," "very stout English lady with a huge crinoline," "lonely French female" . . .

In October 1861, *The Book of Household Management* was finally published, with a publicity campaign that sold the book this way:

A NEW AND PRACTICAL WORK
Adapted for every family
and one that will save money every day
and last a life-time.

The advertising worked well, because the book sold sixty thousand copies in the first year and over two million within the decade.

Bella prided herself on being practical and efficient with words as well as in the kitchen. She is known for having coined certain phrases that are still a common part of our language, such as, "A place for everything and everything in its place."

She had no control over the health of her children, however. At Christmastime in 1862, the second Samuel became ill with scarlet fever—in the days before penicillin—and died at three and a half years.

After a break, while she became busier and more famous due to the book, Bella gave birth on New Year's Eve to a third son, called Orchart, this time taking his father's middle name. He was perfectly healthy, and just a year younger than his uncle, Bella's new and final brother, Horace.

Sixteen months after Orchart was born, in 1865, Bella had her fourth baby, another boy, named Mayson. She was twenty-eight years old. By the next day, Bella was sick with puerperal fever, an illness that used to be sadly common for women who had just given birth. Bella died within a week, leaving two small boys and a heartbroken Sam. Many generations of readers and cooks have benefited from Bella's exuberant scribbling, cut way too short. Even if her name is no longer a household word, her legacy is in every recipe we use to make a meal.

Perhaps the easiest recipe in the book is this favorite dessert, item number 1602:

BOX OF CHOCOLATE
This is served in an ornamental box, placed on a glass plate or dish.

Seasonable: May be purchased at any time.

Among the more than nine hundred recipes in *The Book of Household Management*, Isabella Beeton included suggestions for swans, boar, rabbit, and deer.

Mary Kingsley, however, tasted even more exotic creatures. She had tips for cooking hippopotamus, snake, and crocodile . . .

Mary Kingsley

1862—1900

You are coming home from a long and dangerous beetle-hunt in the
forest; you have battled with mighty beetles the size of pie dishes,
they have flown at your head, got into your hair and then nipped you
smartly. You have been also considerably stung and bitten by flies, ants,
etc., and are most likely sopping wet with rain, or with the wading of
streams, and you are tired and your feet go low along the ground . . .
you then deposit promptly in some prickly ground crop, or against a
tree stump, and then, if there is human blood in you, you say d—n!

ᕒ

M ary Henrietta Kingsley preferred not to write out the full
swear word *damn*, despite having frequent reason to use it.
She was a proper Victorian lady—at least on the outside.
But in her heart she was an explorer and a scientist. She had traveled a
long way to find those giant beetles, at a time when English ladies were
expected to sit sewing quietly beside the fire.

And she didn't stop at beetles. In West Africa, Mary discovered a new
species of fish, ate hippopotamus, waded through swamps, interviewed
witch doctors, climbed a volcanic mountain, and was an overnight guest
in a cannibal village. Whatever her daily perils, Mary wrote long, colorful letters to friends and recorded every detail in her battered bush diary.
She then went home and published two books about her adventures,
introducing the suspicious English audience to her beloved West Africa
and stirring up controversy whenever she opened her mouth.

Mary had little schooling as a child, but she liked to read books from her
father's enormous library, particularly the ones about long sea voyages,

"Most Notorious Pyrates," and far-away places. She did not imagine that some day she would see them for herself.

Her young years were spent in service to her disabled mother, named Mary Bailey, who did not like to be nursed by anyone other than her daughter. The assumption was still common in England, during Mary's life in the late 1800s, that this kind of devotion was what daughters were for. Mary's younger brother, Charley, was sent away to a fancy boarding school, but Mary, being a girl, remained within reach of her mother's bedside. She apparently taught herself to read, and her spelling was always unreliable.

Mary's Uncle Henry was a novelist. Another uncle, Charles Kingsley, wrote a famous children's book called *The Water Babies*. But it was her father, George, who most influenced the direction her life would take. He was a doctor who traveled for most of the year all over the world, attending wealthy gentlemen instead of his own family. From as far away as Egypt, North Africa, the South Pacific Ocean, and the Wild West of America, he wrote letters home, full of thrilling incidents and exotic sights.

When George Kingsley paused briefly in his travels to visit the family, usually as a surprise, his demands for silence and obedience were difficult to satisfy. Mary remembered hiding her pet rooster, Ki Ki, at the bottom of the garden so that her father would not be disturbed by its crowing and could stop hurling books out the window! She did, however, help her father with his research, and she was bitten with the same curiosity about maps and the people who inhabited distant lands. Apart from Mr. Kingsley, there were others writing in this genre: part adventurous travelogue and part serious study of geography, biology, or anthropology. But to Mary's knowledge, the writers were all men, and the only connection they had to her own life of confinement was that they provided a much-needed escape for her imagination.

When it came time for Charley to go to university, the whole family moved to the city of Cambridge, home of one of the finest universities in England. Although women were not then permitted to attend classes there, Mary had friends for the first time in her life and was occasionally in the company of brilliant scholars. But her cranky, ailing, and uneducated mother eventually caused the family to be outcasts in the community. As Mrs. Kingsley got sicker, she lost touch with the world around her. At her death, in 1892 (when her daughter was thirty years old), she likely did not realize that her husband had already died, suddenly in his sleep, just a few weeks before her.

Six years earlier, Queen Victoria had become a widow, and her loss had an enormous impact on the English attitude toward mourning. Three years after her coronation, Victoria had been wed—for love rather than politics—to her cousin, Prince Albert. Albert was clever and handsome and dedicated to many causes for the benefit of the public, such as education, the fight against slavery worldwide, and support for the arts. Just before Christmas in 1861, Prince Albert died from typhoid fever, at the young age of forty-two. Queen Victoria was devastated. She crawled into a lengthy period of mourning and for several years was rarely seen in public. She dressed only in black and grieved for the rest of her life.

This dramatic display of sorrow launched an era of severe mourning regulations and fashions. Anyone with a death in the family, including children and servants, was expected to wear certain attire for months or even years, on a strict timetable. Any glossy material, like satin or fur, was forbidden. Only dull black fabrics were allowed, and jewelry made of a dark stone called jet; black hair ornaments, umbrellas, footwear, and handbags were all required.

Mary Kingsley took these guidelines seriously. Despite her open mind on many other topics, according to a biographer, "she wore mourning all her life," from neckline to hemline, and "she wrote every single letter— and she was a huge letter writer—on black-rimmed notepaper, to mark the death of her parents."

Charley Kingsley expected that his sister would continue to live with and take care of him. Conveniently, he soon departed on a trip to the Far East, and Mary snatched the only chance that she might ever have to follow her own dreams. For as long as she could remember, her life had been focused on caring for other people. "I have always been the doer of odd jobs—and lived in the joys, sorrows, and worries of other people," she wrote in a letter to a friend.

Now she was suddenly in the position of asking herself a question she'd never considered: What do I want to do? The answer was to take a sea voyage to the Canary Islands!

Mary made her arrangements quickly. She wanted to pack as little as possible. She took her black mourning clothes and a "long waterproof sack neatly closed at the top with a bar and handle" stuffed with blankets, boots, and books. Although most of Mary's friends were horrified at her ambitious plans, one of them sent along a book of *Phrases in common use* in Dahomey, one of the West African countries she intended to visit. As Mary describes it:

> The opening sentence . . . was, "Help, I am drowning" . . . and then another cry, "The boat is upset." "Get up, you lazy scamps," is the next exclamation, followed almost immediately by the question, 'Why has not this man been buried?" "It is fetish that has killed him, and he must lie here exposed with nothing on him until only the bones remain," is the cheerful answer.

Fetish was one of the two things that Mary was particularly curious to study in Africa. *Fetish* is the word for an object that is believed to hold magical powers or to be inhabited by a spirit.

Mary's other main interest was fish. Before departing, she met with Dr. Albert Gunther, the resident ichthyologist (fish specialist) at the British Museum. He was delighted by her offer to collect samples of species that were unknown in England.

Mary's friends were either scandalized or frightened by what she planned to do. Women did *not* travel by themselves, especially to dangerous places full of savages! It was well known that foreigners in Africa faced many perils. They often died of tropical diseases, were murdered— even eaten—or were simply never heard from again. The doctors she consulted confirmed that illness and infection were rampant in Africa. "'Deadliest spot on earth,' they said cheerfully, and showed me maps of the geographical distribution of disease."

For the many things that people warned her about, Mary created her own set of categories:

The dangers of West Africa.
The disagreeables of West Africa.
The diseases of West Africa.
The things you must take to West Africa.
The things you find most handy in West Africa.
The worst possible things you can do in West Africa.

A white woman traveling alone was likely to be particularly vulnerable. Mary carried a small revolver as protection, and swore that her sharp little knife would be used upon herself if she were ever in an unbearable situation. Luckily, she was never tested to that extreme. However, Mary realized that her chances of surviving her journey were slim. "I went down to West Africa to die," she later said. "I fully expected to get killed by the local nobility and gentry."

Quite hurriedly, but what felt like *finally*, Mary set sail in the sweltering month of August on a steamship bound for the Canary Islands, off the coast of Morocco. As the boat approached the first port of call, Mary wrote this about the famous Peak of Tenerife: "Whenever and however it may be seen, soft and dream-like in the sunshine, or melodramatic and bizarre in the moonlight, it is one of the most beautiful things the eye of man may see." Her isolated life had now officially opened up to the wide world.

Mary spent several weeks in the Canary Islands and along what she called "the Coast" of West Africa. She soon saw her preconceptions erased and exchanged for eye-opening new lessons. She listened gratefully to the boat captain and the traders who shared their vast knowledge and experience of the country that so compelled her.

She quickly recognized the wisdom of traveling with items of value to the natives. Trading provided a natural overture to people who might otherwise be suspicious. On her future trips, she followed this instinct, bringing knives, fish hooks, mirrors, hair combs, "lucifer matches," perfume, and other desirable items. She learned that exchanging goods and knowledge was a great equalizer among strangers.

When Mary returned to England, she discovered that her brother, Charley, had sold the house she'd always lived in. It fell to Mary to do most of the sorting and packing up of her parents' lives. The Victorian daughter in Mary resigned herself to this sad chore, but when Charley assumed that she would now be a dutiful sister and housekeeper for him, her obedience lasted for only a few months. Mary was busy making plans. In December 1894, she was on the move again, retracing her footsteps via the Canaries back to West Africa. This second voyage, and the next one, in 1895, provided enough adventure for her two long books.

When the steamer stopped at the first African port of call—market day at Freetown in Sierra Leone—Mary's excitement nearly vibrated on the page as she wrote about the streets, paved "in a way more suitable for naked feet, by green Bahama grass," the natives carrying huge burdens on their heads, the noise, the confusion, "and half a hundred other indescribabilia." Eager humor accompanied her observations of bare-breasted women, exotic vegetables and fruits, bolts of bright textiles, whole herds of stray sheep and goats, turkey vultures, "cinnamon-coloured cattle," a dog-faced monkey, an ostrich, "small, lean, lank yellow dogs with very erect ears," and pigs with rings through their noses.

Every single person, place, or thing that Mary saw was utterly different from what she had known in England, and yet she had a strong feeling of kinship with her new surroundings. While traveling she kept extensive notes; her writing style was exuberant, colorful, ungrammatical, and dense with detail. Some of her original journal entries were lifted directly into her books, *Travels in West Africa* and later *West African Studies*. Much more had to be trimmed and edited before it could be published.

Mary's extraordinary intelligence and relentless curiosity meant that she observed, analyzed, and recorded everything she encountered—and went looking for anything that might be hidden from the usual view of a visitor. Through study, and conversation with nearly everyone she met abroad, she became an expert on a mind-boggling range of topics. Unusual for an English person, Mary quickly realized the error of the simplistic assumption that the label *African* could adequately describe the many tribes that she encountered: "African culture, I may remark, varies just the same as European in this, that there is as much difference in the manners of life between, say, an Igalwa and a Bubi of Fernando Po, as there is between a Londoner and a Laplander."

Nothing escaped Mary's analytic notice and sharp-eyed—though sometimes rambling—descriptions: the varieties of architecture and town-planning; the fashions, jewelry, trades, and crafts; marriage and ceremonial customs; geographical information about mangrove swamps, tide patterns, malarial mud; witchcraft and fetish; music; missionaries; initiation; the abject fate of widows; illness and healing. "Next in danger to the diseases come the remedies for them," she wrote. A common topic of conversation seems to have been the high fatality rate of white visitors to Africa. On visiting one cemetery, her guide told her, "'Oh! we always keep two graves ready dug for Europeans. We have to bury very quickly here, you know . . . .'"

She paid attention to the preparation of local delicacies and often included a form of recipe. After explaining the Igalwa tribe's process of making a kind of "cheese" from the kernels of a mango-like fruit, she wrote: "This dish is really excellent, even when made with python, hippo, or crocodile. It makes the former most palatable; but of course it does not remove the musky taste from crocodile; nothing I know of will."

More culinary advice comes later:

The first day in the forest we came across a snake—a beauty with a new red-brown and yellow-patterned velvety skin, about three feet six inches long and as thick as a man's thigh. . . . We had the snake for supper, that is to say the Fan and I; the others would not touch it, although a good snake, properly cooked, is one of the best meats one gets out here, far and away better than the African fowl.

Mary had several unexpected meetings with large African wildlife, usually reported with irony, while minimizing the menace.

For instance:

A crocodile drifting down in deep water, or lying asleep with its jaws open on a sand-bank in the sun, is a picturesque adornment to the landscape when you are on the deck of a steamer, and you can write home about it and frighten your relations on your behalf; but when you are away among the swamps in a small dug-out canoe, and that crocodile and his relations are awake— a thing he makes a point of being at flood tide because of fish coming along . . . you may not be able to write home about him, and you get frightened on your own behalf; for crocodiles can, and often do, in such places, grab at people in small canoes.

As far as elephants were concerned:

I saw . . . wading and rolling in the mud, a herd of five elephants. I remembered, hastily, that your one chance when charged by several elephants is to dodge them round trees, working down wind all the time, until they lose smell and sight of you, then to lie quiet for a time, and go home.

On the subject of gorillas, she was of two opinions. She felt "horrible disgust" for them, but she also said: "I have seen many wild animals in their native wilds, but never have I seen anything to equal gorillas going through bush; it is a graceful, powerful, superbly perfect hand-trapeze performance."

She didn't care that a leopard's whiskers were considered powerful *ju ju* (an amulet against spirits). She had no intention of backing down when she met one face to face: "The leopard crouched, I think to spring on me. I can see its great, beautiful, lambent eyes still, and I seized an earthen water-cooler and flung it straight at them. It was a noble shot; it burst on the leopard's head like a shell and the leopard went for bush."

While traveling upstream as the only passenger on a boat called the *Eclaireur*, Mary reported a dramatic episode concerning the retrieval of the floating corpse of a dead hippopotamus. Afterwards, although the task of cutting up their catch was extremely unpleasant, "for remember that hippo had been dead and in the warm river-water for more than a week," Mary bravely tried yet another new taste sensation: "Hippo flesh is not to be despised by black man or white; I have enjoyed it far more than the stringy beef or vapid goat's flesh one gets down here."

As well as menacing wild animals, Mary and her guides faced endless other discomforts and dangers. After a wet and dangerous passage through an underground river, she wrote that "our souls, unliberated by funeral rites from this world, would have to hover for ever over the Ogowé near the scene of our catastrophe. I own this idea was an unpleasant one—fancy having to pass the day in those caves with the bats, and then come out and wander all night in the cold mists!"

They crossed several swamps: "We were two hours and a quarter passing that swamp. . . . One and all, we got horribly infested with leeches, having a frill of them round our necks like astrakhan collars, and our hands covered with them, when we came out." And endured sweltering heat: "My face and particularly my lips are a misery to me, having been blistered all over by yesterday's sun . . ."

All this plus torrential rain, countless dunks in rivers, and several tumbles down rocks—Mary met the physical obstacles and hardships with astonishing grace and good spirits. "I just take a flying slide of twenty feet or so and shoot, flump, under the tree on my back, and then deliberate whether it is worth while getting up again to go on with such a world; but vanity forbids my dying like a dog in a ditch, and I scramble up . . ."

In one region, Mary and her fellow passengers encountered the worst insects so far. "Conversation and atmosphere are full of mosquitoes," she noted. "I retired into my cabin, so as to get under the mosquito curtains to write."

Not even rumors of cannibal tribes put Mary off pursuing her passion for both fish and fetish. Her journey through uncharted territory, up the Ogowé River, would teach her plenty about both, but even more about cannibals.

In her writings, Mary referred to the Fan people, though their name was actually Fang. She was protecting their reputation; by leaving off the final letter, her favorite tribe would not appear so fearful to her readers. Right from the start, Mary's time among the Fang was eventful. She was walking ahead of her guides, knowing that they would soon catch up to her slower pace.

> . . . the next news was I was in a heap, on a lot of spikes, some fifteen feet or so below ground level, at the bottom of a bag-shaped game pit. It is at these times you realize the blessing of a good thick skirt. Had I paid heed to the advice of many people in England . . . and adopted masculine garments, I should have been spiked to the bone, and done for. Whereas, save for a good many bruises, here I was with the fullness of my skirt tucked under me, sitting on nine ebony spikes some twelve inches long, in comparative comfort, howling lustily to be hauled out.

After some initial suspicion, the villagers welcomed Mary and her company, with the chief even moving out of his own little house to allow Mary to sleep there. "I shook hands with and thanked the chief," wrote Mary. "And directed that all the loads should be placed inside the huts. I must admit my good friend was a villainous-looking savage, but he behaved most hospitably and kindly."

During the night, however, Mary was disturbed by an unpleasant smell that she tracked to one of the small bags suspended from the ceiling. She carefully noted the manner in which the bag was tied, so that she could refasten it afterwards. "I then shook its contents out in my hat, for fear of losing anything of value. They were a human hand, three big toes, four eyes, two ears, and other portions of the human frame. The hand was fresh, the others only so so, and shrivelled."

Apparently, Mary discovered, "although the Fans will eat their fellow friendly tribesfolk, yet they like to keep a little something belonging to them as a memento." As grim as this discovery was, she did not feel threatened by the habits of her hosts:

The cannibalism of the Fans, although a prevalent habit, is no danger, I think, to white people, except as regards the bother it gives one in preventing one's black companions from getting eaten. The Fan is not a cannibal from sacrificial motives like the negro. He does it in his common sense way. Man's flesh, he says, is good to eat, very good, and he wishes you would try it.

If cannibals weren't treacherous enough, there were certainly other dangers awaiting Mary and her band of guides, especially as they considered what would be their greatest challenge: the ascent of Mount Cameroon. There were frequent occasions for resourcefulness while bush trekking; when they ran out of palm oil for treating their boots, for instance, Mary used animal fat instead. During the climb of Mount Cameroon, the company did not bring enough water with them—possibly a trick of the guides to force Mary to abandon the effort. Mary wrote, "The rain now began to fall, thank goodness, and I drew the thick ears of grass through my parched lips." Later, "we limp in, our feet sore with rugged rocks, and everything we have on, or in the loads, wringing wet, save the matches, which providentially I had put into my soap-box."

Mount Cameroon is locally called Mungo or Mongo ma Ndemi, "Mountain of Greatness." It is an active volcano and the highest peak in West Africa, within sight of the Atlantic Ocean, when not shrouded in fog. Some of the heaviest rainfall in the world occurs in this region. Mary was possibly the first woman, and certainly the first white woman, to climb it. But it was far from easy, especially in an ankle-length skirt!

Mary was on this part of the trek with an odd collection of young men, to whom, writing in her journal, she gave descriptive nicknames like "Blue Jacket" and "Windbag." Although they were meant to be leading her, she seems to have had an almost motherly relationship with them: "I believe if I had collapsed too—the cold tempted me to do so as nothing else can—they would have lain down and died in the cold sleety rain."

Mary does not tell us much about her writing habits, but partway up the mountain, she mentioned this: "I write by the light of an insect-haunted lantern, sitting on the bed, which is tucked in among the trees some twenty yards away from the boys' fire. There is a bird whistling in a deep rich note that I have never heard before."

Mary records one bumbling incident after another: crashing rainstorms, missing supplies, drenched campsites and beds, and lost or frightened guides. The "boys" were reluctant to attempt the final push for the summit, but of course Mary had not come that far to turn back without trying. As she neared the top alone, she was greeted by:

> . . . a burst of bitter wind, and a sheet of blinding, stinging rain. I make my way up through it towards a peak which I soon see through a tear in the mist is not the highest, so I angle off and go up the one to the left, and after a desperate fight reach the cairn—only, alas! to find a hurricane raging and a fog in full possession, and not a ten yards' view to be had in any direction. . . . Verily I am no mountaineer, for there is in me no exultation, but only a deep disgust because the weather has robbed me of my main object in coming here, namely to get a good view. . . . I took my chance and it failed, so there's nothing to complain about.

Descending from the mountain was every bit as dramatic as going up, with several perilous moments while dismally lost or soaking wet or teetering over chasms. "'Don't fall,' I yelled which was the only good advice I could think of to give them just then."

But always the Englishwoman shone through: "Head man and I get out the hidden demijohn of rum, and the beef and rice, and I serve out a tot of rum each to the boys, who are shivering dreadfully, waiting for Cook to get the fire. He soon does this, and then I have my hot tea and the men their hot food . . ." Mary's gratitude conquers all discomfort whenever she mentions "having her tea."

Mary felt huge affection and respect for the many Africans that she met and traveled with and lived with in their homeland. She paid attention to what they related about their customs, and faithfully reported in her books what her experience and studies had taught her.

Before her first book was published, even before she had set foot back in her own country, tales of Mary Kingsley's exploits had reached England. She became quite a celebrity, and much in demand as a speaker. Her strong opinions, such as objecting to the common notion that the African brain was somehow not fully formed, were scrutinized and discussed by the public. She argued that a "black man is no more an undeveloped white man than a rabbit is an undeveloped hare." She suggested that the Africans should be left alone to their own religious life and not forcibly converted to Christianity. She resented the European notion that the African way of life could be replaced with what she called "their own rubbishy white culture."

Even more controversial was her distress about the harmful impact that King Leopold II of Belgium was having in the Belgian Congo. Nearly twenty years earlier, in 1878, Leopold had hired the celebrated explorer Henry Morton Stanley to make an expedition along the Congo River. Knowing that England and other countries would object to his real motives, Leopold pretended that Stanley was merely furthering his previous ventures in the region. However, on Leopold's behalf and using trinkets and bolts of cloth as currency, Stanley negotiated treaties with 450 tribal chiefs, following his king's orders that the agreements should be as "brief as possible and in a couple of articles must grant us everything." Leopold now had the right to take control of the prosperous trading of rubber and ivory in the region. He enslaved, mistreated, and killed between 5 and 8 million of the native inhabitants.

Belgium was certainly not the only country to exploit the African people. Portugal and Spain, among others, had been doing it for centuries, with the United States being a more recent transgressor. But it was the atrocities resulting from Leopold's presence in the Congo that Mary Kingsley witnessed—among the few events so terrible that she could *not* bring herself to discuss at length what she'd seen. But she provided the sort of eyewitness testimony that activists could use in their battle against the horror and injustice being perpetrated by King Leopold's colonization.

In a rare understatement, Mary's simple opinion was that "the African at large . . . has been mismanaged of late years by the white races."

As outspoken as she was on behalf of African rights, Mary was *opposed* to the struggle in England for women's suffrage. Ironically, she spoke firmly against women being members of academic societies and sneered at the idea that they should have the right to vote.

One personal result of Mary's travels was that she kept her fire burning at such a rate that her English house maintained tropical temperatures at all times. Her visitors found it stifling, but to her it felt like home.

Mary Kingsley traveled to Africa one last time, in 1900, seven years after her parents' death. She was thirty-eight years old. This time she went as a nurse, to care for soldiers during the Boer War in South Africa. She herself caught typhoid fever. Knowing that she was dying, Mary asked that she be buried at sea, recalling a paragraph she'd written in the introduction to *Travels in West Africa* years earlier:

> You hear, nearer to you than the voices of the people round, nearer than the roar of the city traffic, the sound of the surf that is breaking on the shore down there, and the sound of the wind talking on the hard palm leaves and the thump of the natives' tom-toms; or the cry of the parrots passing over the mangrove swamps in the evening time; or the sweet, long, mellow whistle of the plantain warblers calling up the dawn; and everything that is round you grows poor and thin in the face of the vision, and you want to go back to the Coast that is calling you, saying, as the African says to the departing soul of his dying friend, "Come back, come back, this is your home."

Although Mary's wish was carried out, it was reported that "the coffin, wrongly weighted, bobbed indomitably on the surface. A party of men had to row out, and complete the funeral. It was a touch of cussedness she might have enjoyed."

Mary Kingsley was an adventurer and a writer, displaying the same qualities in both professions: a unique, enthusiastic approach, great wit, and a willingness to do what had not been tried before.

"One by one I took my old ideas derived from books and thoughts based on imperfect knowledge and weighed them against the real life around me, and found them either worthless or wanting."

Mary Kingsley fell passionately in love with West Africa, but perhaps even more so with the notion of travel as a way to uncover new ideas.

Nellie Bly, more than most other women in history, was an example of someone determined to expose the truth—and she traveled around the world as part of that plan . . .

Nellie Bly

1864–1922

My teeth chattered and my limbs were goose-fleshed and blue with cold. Suddenly I got, one after the other, three buckets of water over my head—ice-cold water, too—into my eyes, my ears, my nose and my mouth. I think I experienced some of the sensations of a drowning person as they dragged me, gasping, shivering and quaking, from the tub. For once I did look insane. . . . They put me, dripping wet, into a short canton flannel slip, labeled across the extreme end in large black letters, "Lunatic Asylum, B. I H. 6." The letters meant Blackwell's Island, Hall 6.

❧

This description of bath time in the asylum turned Nellie Bly into a national celebrity. She had set out to prove to the newspaper world that a woman could be a serious journalist. She went several steps further with the publication of this article exposing the treatment of mentally ill patients in New York City. Nellie, often described as the first undercover reporter, became a brilliant overnight sensation.

Nellie's real name was Elizabeth Jane Cochrane. Legend has it that she was nicknamed "Pink" after being christened in a bright pink gown. She was born in Pittsburg, in 1864, before the city added an "h" to the end of its name.

Pink's father was a judge, but he died when she was six. Her mother, Mary Jane, chose the usual route for widows in those days: she got married again in order to provide a home for her children. Horribly, Mary Jane's second husband drank too much and was abusive to his new wife. Mary Jane summoned up her courage and filed for divorce. In those days, divorce was uncommon and carried a heavy burden of shame. Pink was then fourteen, the second of five siblings. She and her older brother Albert testified at the divorce trial, describing aloud the painful scenes they'd witnessed.

Was this when Pink first realized that well-used words could get results? She certainly understood the importance of being employed and self-reliant, especially for a woman. She swore never to depend on a man's support instead of making her own living.

Although Pink was still young by today's standards, she shed her childhood nickname and went excitedly to study at a teachers' college, then called a "normal school." But after one term there were no funds to continue; she came home to face the reality of being an impoverished woman.

Mary Jane moved her family frequently during Elizabeth's teen years. As the money ran out, the lodgings became bleaker and shabbier. Their fellow tenants were often divorced women, struggling to pay their way in a world that did not yet value females as part of the work force.

In 1885, when Elizabeth was eighteen, she read a newspaper column in the *Pittsburg Dispatch* written by someone whose pen name was the "Quiet Observer." One piece was titled *What Girls Are Good For*. The writer was dismayed at the number of "restless, dissatisfied females" applying for jobs in stores and businesses. He claimed that women should work at making the "home a little paradise." His opinion in another column was that "there is no greater abnormality than a woman in breeches, unless it is a man in petticoats."

Infuriated, Elizabeth sat down and wrote an emphatic protest to the editor, speaking up on behalf of the young ladies she knew who were striving to improve their circumstances. She signed her letter "Lonely Orphan Girl."

The editor, a man named George A. Madden, was impressed with her self-assured voice—in spite of her sloppy grammar—but did not publish the letter. Who was this brash and opinionated writer? Assuming that the "Lonely Orphan Girl" was a man, George printed a request that the fellow contact the newspaper.

Elizabeth snatched the opportunity and showed up at the *Dispatch* office in person. Newspaper rooms back then were dominated by men, noisy from the printing presses rumbling on the floor below, and often filled with tobacco smoke. When Elizabeth stepped in, with her petite figure, sweet face, and bright brown eyes, the entire staff must have stopped to stare. George was flabbergasted at her self-assurance and decided to give her a chance.

He hired her to write a story about "the woman's sphere." Elizabeth was paid five dollars, and George personally edited the piece, probably to make sure all the grammar got corrected. Her first appearance in print, with a piece called "The Girl Puzzle," foreshadowed her interests for years to come. She chastised men and privileged women for not recognizing the obstacles faced by ordinary working girls, those "without talent, without beauty, without money." She suggested that wealthy readers consider how the amount of money they spent on their dogs might, in a poorer household, have "paid father's doctor bill, bought mother a new dress, shoes for the little ones, and imagine how nice it would be could baby have the beef tea that is made for your favorite pug, or the care and kindness that is bestowed upon it."

Elizabeth also wondered why clever and industrious girls could not be employed as young men were, starting as messengers in a company, and working their way up? "Just as smart and a great deal quicker to learn; why, then, can they not do the same?" She thought girls would make good train conductors, too. Why not?

Elizabeth told her editor that next she'd like to write about divorce. George reluctantly agreed, and she set to work on the article called "Mad Marriages," calling for changes to the Pennsylvania divorce laws. She had her mother's situation in mind when she suggested, among other things, that drunkards should not be permitted to marry without full disclosure of their wretched lifestyle.

Whether or not Madden believed in women working, he was smart enough to know that a whiff of scandal was good business. His business was to sell newspapers, and this girl's stories were going to do just that.

George wanted to find a better pen name for his new writer than "Lonely Orphan Girl," but of course "Elizabeth Cochrane" wouldn't do, either; no lady would willingly let her real name be seen in print. There was a popular song at the time about a girl named Nelly Bly. That was the name they chose to go down in history.

Although he was a little worried about hiring an eighteen- year-old girl to cover gritty subjects, George offered Nellie a regular job for five dollars a week. She accepted at once. She wanted to write about the factories of her own city. George told her to go ahead, and out spilled a colorful eight-part series titled "Our Workshop Girls: Women's Labor in Pittsburg."

These articles were not, as some reports have claimed, a scorching exposé of the appalling conditions in Pittsburg's manufacturing world, but they represent the first discussion of a subject that mattered to Nellie all of her life. As a young reporter, she did not yet dig deep, but she visited the factories, and interviewed the employed girls and women about their lives after work as well as on the assembly line, covering in detail a slice of life not usually mentioned in print.

George raised Nellie's pay to ten dollars a week and made her the "Society Editor," covering so-called "women's topics" like gardening advice and fashion updates. She was bored silly, and begged her boss to give her something with more substance.

It took a year before she convinced George to let her write again about serious issues. She finished an article about the prison system, and then had the idea to masquerade as a factory girl, to learn "from the inside" what that life was like. Dressed in shabby clothing, Nellie went out looking for a job. Despite having no training or useful skills, she was hired at the first place she applied, a dimly lit factory where the workers hitched cables together under the supervision of a threatening, foul-mouthed foreman. The girls suffered from headaches and bleeding hands, and could be fined for talking. Nellie was fired when she left the assembly line to get a drink of water.

When the articles about the jails and the cable factory were published, the newspaper's circulation went up, but so did the number of furious complaints. George raised Nellie's pay again, and sent her back to look after the ladies' pages.

Frustrated and bored, Nellie decided to go to Mexico and write reports from there. George didn't like the idea one bit. She was a woman, after all, and Mexico was dangerous. Nellie said she'd take her mother and call it a vacation. She would send her stories as she wrote them and George could publish them or not. She claimed she didn't care.

Nellie and her mother took the train all the way to Mexico. And though Nellie did not speak any Spanish, and often found the food "detestable," her notepad was full of scribbled material. She looked at Mexican factories and poverty, but also at fashions, festivals, funerals, horses, sombreros, museums, bullfights, tortilla sellers, sculptors, tombs, ruins, and the customs for courtship and marriage. She got herself in trouble when she began to poke her nose into politics, and she was encouraged to leave the country.

Back home after five months, Pittsburg felt too small. One day, she simply did not show up for work. No one knew where she was until her colleague, Erasmus Wilson, who was the "Quiet Observer" found her note:

DEAR Q.O.—I am off for New York. Look out for me. BLY

When Nellie arrived in New York City in 1886, the Statue of Liberty was one year old, the Brooklyn Bridge was three, and Nellie was twenty-one. She had traveled a little, her writing voice had gained confidence, and she was never afraid to ask questions. But in the big city, she had trouble finding work. No one was interested in hiring a woman. She lost her purse one afternoon in Central Park and lost all her savings. Nearly penniless, she was getting desperate.

Her next bright idea came when she received a letter from a fan—though perhaps that was a made-up excuse. A young woman asked whether she thought New York was the best place to start out as a reporter. Nellie pitched the concept to the *Pittsburg Dispatch*. How did the top newspaper editors in New York City feel about women journalists? In the name of research, Nellie approached the very men she hoped would hire her. Their responses were disheartening; most of them claimed that women either couldn't or shouldn't take on the kind of news that made the front page. It was also said that "women have a problem with accuracy." The story received a tiny ripple of interest, but she still didn't have a job or any money.

She wanted most to work for The World, published by Joseph Pulitzer. Colonel John Cockerill, whom she had met with for her article, was the editor there. According to her version, Nellie borrowed car fare from her landlady and rode to the newspaper building in Park Row. She claims that she convinced the guards to let her up to Cockerill's office, bringing along her clippings and several bold ideas for new stories. Cockerill did not hire her at once, but he was intrigued enough to pay her twenty-five dollars not to go to another paper while he thought about it—and probably discussed the matter with his publisher, the renowned Mr. Pulitzer.

A couple of male reporters had pulled off occasional episodes of "stunt" or "detective" reporting, but no woman had tried it yet. One of Nellie's proposals was to go to Europe and to sail back in steerage, pretending to be an immigrant, to give readers a real feeling of the experience. The World decided that was too big an assignment for a newcomer, but there had been recent rumblings about the treatment of mental patients at the local asylum. Could Nellie pretend to be insane? Perhaps she could get herself committed to the institution on Blackwell's Island off the edge of Manhattan?

Nellie jumped on the idea. There was nothing she liked better than a crusade. "I said I could and I would. And I did . . . I took upon myself to enact the part of a poor, unfortunate crazy girl, and felt it my duty not to shirk any of the disagreeable results that should follow."

The World requested that she use the name Nellie Brown so they could identify her when the time came to have her released, but until then the plan was up to Nellie. She devised how to get herself committed and how she would convince the doctors of her insanity.

On the morning of her departure, "tenderly I put my tooth-brush aside, and, when taking a final rub of the soap, I murmured, 'It may be for days, and it may be for longer.' Then I donned the old clothing I had selected for the occasion."

Her first stop was a boarding house. "From a directory I selected the Temporary Home for Females, No. 84 Second Avenue." There were several other girls with rooms in this place, and they all ate together under the eye of the matron. Nellie wrote a detailed account of how she acted crazy at mealtimes, pretending to be disoriented and staging occasional outbursts. After two nights, the police were called and she was taken to the Essex Market Police Courtroom, whence she was sent on to Bellevue Hospital. At Bellevue she had her first glimpse of the treatment she could expect for the rest of her experiment. At suppertime she was given "a small tin plate on which was a piece of boiled meat and a potato. It could not have been colder had it been cooked the week before, and it had no chance to make acquaintance with salt or pepper."

She did not have misgivings exactly, but, "In spite of the knowledge of my sanity and the assurance that I would be released in a few days, my heart gave a sharp twinge. Pronounced insane by four expert doctors and shut up behind the unmerciful bolts and bars of a madhouse! Not to be confined alone, but to be a companion, day and night, of senseless, chattering lunatics; to sleep with them, to eat with them, to be considered one of them, was an uncomfortable position."

Nellie was committed to the asylum on Blackwell's Island and taken there by boat with several other women.

"But here let me say one thing: From the moment I entered the insane ward on the Island, I made no attempt to keep up the assumed role of insanity. I talked and acted just as I do in ordinary life. Yet, strange to say, the more sanely I talked and acted, the crazier I was thought to be . . ." Not quite as she talked in real life, actually. She pretended that she was from Cuba and spoke erratic English, but otherwise behaved normally.

The first supper on the island was five prunes, a saucer of pale tea, and a slice of bread with rancid butter. Then, after the frightening and humiliating ice-bath, it was time for bed. Nellie noticed that the long minutes it took to lock or unlock all the cells would be quite dangerous in case of a fire. When she suggested to a doctor that all the locked rooms be opened with the turn of a single crank at the end of a hallway, he assumed at once that she must have been in a prison where such locks existed.

According to Nellie, breakfast was disgusting:

> I was hungry, but the food would not down. I asked for unbuttered bread and was given it. I cannot tell you of anything that is the same dirty, black color. It was hard, and in places nothing more than dried dough. I found a spider in my slice, so I did not eat it. I tried the oatmeal and molasses, but it was wretched, and so I endeavored, but without much show of success, to choke down the tea.

It didn't help that "In our short walks we passed the kitchen where food was prepared for the nurses and doctors. There we got glimpses of melons and grapes and all kinds of fruits, beautiful white bread and nice meats, and the hungry feeling would be increased tenfold."

Despite being better fed, the nurses were not kind: "I came in and saw Miss Grady with my note-book and long lead pencil, bought just for the occasion. 'I want my book and pencil,' I said, quite truthfully. 'It helps me remember things.' I was very anxious to get it to make notes in and was disappointed when she said: 'You can't have it, so shut up.'" When Nellie later asked a doctor to have the items returned to her, "I was advised to fight against the imaginations of my brain."

Even without her pencil and notebook, Nellie managed to recall the entire residence on Blackwell Island in remarkable detail. Her experience with Nurse Grady was mild compared to that of a fellow prisoner, who described her treatment this way:

> "For crying the nurses beat me with a broom-handle and jumped on me, injuring me internally, so that I shall never get over it. Then they tied my hands and feet, and, throwing a sheet over my head, twisted it tightly around my throat, so I could not scream, and thus put me in a bathtub filled with cold water. They held me under until I gave up every hope and became

senseless. At other times they took hold of my ears and beat my head on the floor and against the wall. Then they pulled out my hair by the roots, so that it will never grow in again."

When it was time to wash their faces in the morning, Nellie realized that all forty-five women in Hall 6 were sharing two towels. "I went to the bathtub and washed my face at the running faucet and my under-skirt did duty for a towel."

Nellie made several friends among the other inmates—women who were also clearly not insane, but imprisoned because they did not speak English well, or perhaps were exhausted and temporarily depressed by difficult lives. She found it hard not to laugh during their first walk, a parade of lunatics in white straw sunbonnets: "Can you imagine the sight? According to one of the physicians there are 1,600 insane women on Blackwell's Island."

Nellie was certain that some of those women had not become crazy until they'd got to the asylum. The doctors were quite able, she said, "to take a perfectly sane and healthy woman, shut her up and make her sit from 6 A. M. until 8 P. M. on straight-back benches, not allow her to talk or move during these hours, give her no reading and let her know nothing of the world or its doings, give her bad food and harsh treatment, and see how long it will take to make her insane. Two months would make her a mental and physical wreck."

Most of the miserable patients on Blackwell's Island had been forgotten by the outside world, but the appearance of the pretty Nellie Brown, a mystery woman with amnesia, had caught the attention of the press. Nellie was alarmed one day to be pushed into a room where a reporter was waiting in the hope of learning her identity. The young man was someone Nellie knew, and he recognized her at once. She begged him not to expose her, knowing it would ruin the story. He agreed and went away.

Finally, after ten days, Nellie was told that someone had arrived to take her home. She was released into the care of a reporter from *The World*, who pretended to be a concerned friend. Nellie's articles were published in two parts by the newspaper and later as a book, *Ten Days in a Madhouse*. Nellie was instantly famous across the country, and the asylum management was mortified.

A committee that had been slowly looking into making improvements at the facility on Blackwell's Island sped up discussions and agreed to provide substantial funds. Within a month, Nellie was invited to join a tour of public inspectors. Changes had already occurred; the women were being re-evaluated, evil nurses had been fired, the food and bedding were far better, and plans were underway to provide activities and improved general care.

Nellie was twenty-three years old and on top of the world. Her mother moved from Pittsburg to New York to live with her daughter. For a while, her sister Kate came along, too.

Nellie followed up her madhouse story with several more where disguise was necessary. She pretended to be an out-of-work maid, with the aim of criticizing dodgy employment agencies. She posed as an unwed mother looking to place her child, in order to expose a black market that sold newborn babies. She got herself hired as a "white slave" in a paper box factory, revealing the underside of modern manufacturing.

Today, this kind of undercover journalism would be frowned on or even considered illegal, but in those days, it was simply part of the competition between sparring newspapers. Anyone plucky enough to pull off a successful stunt was considered a celebrity. Nellie was a star.

She posed as a sinner seeking redemption, to look into the Magdalen Home for Unfortunate Women. She participated in a sting of businessman Edward Phelps, who was bribing New York politicians to vote or not vote on various bills. She exposed the inexperience of the doctors in the free medical clinics where the poor went for consultation. She also wrote some light-hearted stories, about taking ballet lessons and a stint as a chorus girl, and she published an interview with the Wild West showman Buffalo Bill.

Letters began to arrive at *The World* with suggestions of stories for their daredevil reporter to tackle. One of these was the rumor that a man in Central Park was attacking young women. Nellie used herself as bait, of course, and her exposé resulted in the arrest of a carriage driver and the dismissal of police officers who had accepted bribes of beer to ignore the women's complaints.

After this adventure, in 1889, Nellie tried her hand at fiction, writing a novel called *The Mystery of Central Park,* but it did not make much of a splash. Nellie's strength was as a reporter.

Nellie was too busy to have many friends, and she didn't trust the new crop of female reporters who were now hot on the trail of her position and fame. She liked being considered a lady and didn't think much of feminists—or "suffragists," as they were called then, as they fought for women's suffrage, the right to vote. But she interviewed a lawyer named Belva Lockwood, who in 1888 was running for President as a candidate for the National Equal Rights Party. Belva believed that women teachers and other professionals should be paid as much as men. She also wanted world peace and strong limits to the use of alcohol. This was Belva's second try for the White House, but she had little chance of winning: women would not be able to vote in the United States for another forty-two years.

All this was a warm-up for Nellie's next—and last—ambitious stunt. She claimed the idea was all hers, but even if that's not true, it was a good one.

It was my custom to think up ideas on Sunday and lay them before my editor for his approval or disapproval on Monday. But ideas did not come that day and three o'clock in the morning found me weary and with an aching head tossing about in my bed. At last tired and provoked at my slowness in finding a subject, something for the week's work, I thought fretfully:

"I wish I was at the other end of the earth!"

"And why not?" the thought came: "I need a vacation; why not take a trip around the world?"

Around the World in Eighty Days was then a popular novel, written by the Frenchman Jules Verne and published in English about fifteen years earlier. The hero, Phileas Fogg, sets out, on a bet, to encircle the globe in eighty days. Nellie proposed (after spending a morning at a steamship company to make certain it could be done) that she attempt to beat this fictional record and make the journey in seventy-five. This was fourteen years before Orville Wright first flew an airplane in 1903. Long-distance travel was done by steamship or train. The same itinerary today, with the advantage of flight, could probably be accomplished in under four days.

The World publisher, Joseph Pulitzer, argued that, being a woman, Nellie would need to take too much luggage, as well as a chaperon. It would be simpler to send a male reporter instead. Nellie was swift to protest: "'Very well,' I said angrily, 'Start the man, and I'll start the same day for some other newspaper and beat him.'"

Pulitzer considered the idea for about a year until he was suddenly spurred on by news that a young theatrical producer was planning a similar venture. He summoned Nellie and gave her three days to prepare for the assignment of her life.

"I always have a comfortable feeling that nothing is impossible if one applies a certain amount of energy in the right direction," she later said, referring to the effort involved in making the last-minute preparations. She knew that her packing was of the utmost importance. Here is her list, in her own words:

> I was able to pack two traveling caps, three veils, a pair of slippers, a complete outfit of toilet articles, ink-stand, pens, pencils, and copy-paper, pins, needles and thread, a dressing gown, a tennis blazer, a small flask and a drinking cup, several complete changes of underwear, a liberal supply of handkerchiefs . . . and most bulky and uncompromising of all, a jar of cold cream to keep my face from chapping in the varied climates I should encounter.

In her pocket she carried a watch showing the New York hour, while her wristwatch would be changed to suit whatever local time she was traveling in. She also carried a special passport signed by the

Secretary of State, but not the revolver suggested by friends. "I had such a strong belief in the world's greeting me as I greeted it, that I refused to arm myself."

She barely had time to get nervous, until the morning of her departure. "Then to encourage myself I thought, as I was on my way to the ship: 'It's only a matter of 28,000 miles, and seventy-five days and four hours, until I shall be back again.'"

She left American shores on November 14, 1889, from Jersey City on the steamer *Augusta Victoria*, ten minutes and six seconds later than scheduled. Every minute was going to count, but that was only the first of many delays over the next few weeks. Her mother was there to wave her off, as well as an official timekeeper and a reporter from *The World*, who would announce the expedition in that day's paper. Hardly anyone else knew Nellie was leaving, because they wanted the stunt kept a secret until after she'd sailed.

Within minutes she was seasick, and she had to excuse herself three times from the captain's dinner table that night, but after an extremely long sleep—until four o'clock the following afternoon—Nellie adjusted to shipboard life. "I think it is only natural for travelers to take an innocent pleasure in studying the peculiarities of their fellow companions." So that's what she did, for the seven days it took to cross the Atlantic, writing brief character sketches of her shipmates, including a Skye terrier named Home Sweet Home.

Upon arriving at Southampton, England, the pace of Nellie's journey picked up. A tugboat chugged out to meet the steamer, to carry Nellie to an awaiting mail train to London. The English correspondent for *The World* greeted her with the news that Jules Verne himself had invited Nellie to visit his home in Amiens, France. It would mean going without sleep for two nights to get there and still make her ongoing connection, but Nellie was happily willing. She paused in London to send a cable back to the New York office. "I'm alright," it said. "Letter follows." Then she let them know that she was altering the planned itinerary just a little.

The main difficulty in keeping Nellie's exploits on the front page was going to be that of communication. There were no television cameras to follow her from place to place. There were no trans-Atlantic telephones, and the Internet would not exist for another century. So Nellie's news would be sent by telegraph in a few expensive words, or, irregularly, by letter. Her first story was printed seventeen days after her departure. *The World* had to devise other ploys to keep readers interested. They announced a Nellie Bly Guessing Game, offering a free trip to Europe for whoever came closest to guessing the exact time of Nellie's arrival home. Throughout her travels, the number of papers sold increased daily.

Nellie's detour to visit the Verne house was a highlight of the trip: "Jules Verne's bright eyes beamed on me with interest and kindliness, and Mme. Verne greeted me with the cordiality of a cherished friend." Nellie was given a tour of the great man's tidy study and a peek at his current manuscript. She was amazed by the neat erasures and lack of scribbled additions, "which gave me the idea that M. Verne always improved his work by taking out superfluous things and never by adding. One bottle of ink and one penholder was all that shared the desk with the manuscript."

Differing slightly from the route taken by Phileas Fogg, as Nellie told M. Verne:

> "My line of travel is from New York to London, then Calais, Brindisi, Port Said, Ismailia, Suez, Aden, Colombo, Penang, Singapore, Hong Kong, Yokohama, San Francisco, New York."
>
> "If you do it in seventy-nine days, I shall applaud with both hands," Jules Verne said . . . as his glass tipped mine: "Good luck, Nellie Bly."

She had to hurry to catch her train, but she made it, and journeyed on through France and foggy Italy to meet another steamer that would carry her to Ceylon (now known as Sri Lanka). Nellie continued her commentary with complaints about her cabin and the food, as well as vivid specifics about other aspects of the voyage: "Occasionally we would have a dance on deck to the worst music it has ever been my misfortune to hear. The members of the band also washed the dishes."

They paused at Port Said in Egypt, where "before the boat anchored the men armed themselves with canes, to keep off the beggars they said; and the women carried parasols for the same purpose." And, sure enough, "hardly had the anchor dropped than the ship was surrounded with a fleet of small boats, steered by half-clad Arabs, fighting, grabbing, pulling, yelling in their mad haste to be first."

Nellie tended to see the sights from a distinctly American vantage point, comparing everything to what she knew from home. Her attitude toward the native people of other lands was often condescending, and her judgments today seem insensitive. But she was racing against time and did not have the luxury of experiencing other cultures in any depth.

The steamer *Victoria* proceeded down the Suez Canal, a man-made waterway that had opened twenty years earlier to connect the Red Sea and the Mediterranean; 120 miles (192 kilometers) long, it was a massive engineering project that Nellie had been keen to see for herself. It seems to have been a little disappointing: "what looked like an enormous ditch, enclosed on either side with high sand banks."

Next stop was Aden, part of what is now called Yemen, where Nellie swore that the "black fellows have the finest teeth of any mortals." Upon enquiry, she learned that their secret was particular "tree branches of a soft, fibrous wood which they cut into pieces three and four inches in length. With one end of this stick, scraped free of the bark, they rub and polish their teeth until they are perfect in their whiteness." Nellie purchased several sticks for her own use and found them much superior to "the tooth-destroying brush used in America."

These same fellows dyed their hair by bleaching it with a cap of lime, which they wore for several days. This fashion did not extend to the women, who were quite plain by comparison.

In Colombo, the port of Ceylon, Nellie had a two-day delay while awaiting transport to Singapore. She distracted herself by shopping, sending cables to New York, and experimenting with various modes of local transport. She later wrote that, along with steamer and train, she had tried mule, rickshaw, bullock cart, catamaran, sampan, and "half a dozen other conveyances peculiar to Eastern countries."

In Singapore, more precious time ticked by while Nellie waited for the *Oriental* steamer to show up from its previous tour. She hopped over to China during the pause, and bought a short-tailed monkey whom she named McGinty.

When the *Oriental* finally sailed, Nellie was in good spirits, and, despite their late arrival, the steamship *Oceanic* was waiting in the port at Hong Kong to take her back to America. But there, in the steamship company offices, she heard bad news.

"You are going to be beaten," she was told. She'd been challenged to a race, without knowing it. The editors of *Cosmopolitan Magazine* in New York had sent out their own female reporter on the evening of Nellie's departure from New Jersey. Elizabeth Bisland was circling the globe in the opposite direction, and as of that hour was two days ahead, having arrived on the *Oceanic* from America after a record Pacific crossing.

But the crew was determined to give Nellie a fair chance. They sailed from Hong Kong on December 28. They left Japan on January 7 and chugged toward Nellie's deadline, knowing they had to reach the American west coast within ten days so that she'd have time to cross the country by train. Someone wrote a vow on the engine room wall:

For Nellie Bly
We'll do or die.
January 20, 1890

Two days out, the *Oceanic* faced a ferocious monsoon, but made up some speed after the storm and arrived in San Francisco on Day 68, only twenty-four hours behind schedule. A band played on the dock at 7:30 in the morning, among hundreds of well-wishing fans. Also awaiting was more bad news. A blizzard had obliterated the tracks of Nellie's intended rail route, as well as delaying the trainload of reporters who were meant to be covering her arrival back on American soil. But the train company eagerly offered to arrange a special train on an alternate itinerary.

At nine o'clock, Nellie waved good-bye to San Francisco, accompanied by John Jennings, the reporter whom Pulitzer had proposed sending on this world tour instead of her. John had hiked on snowshoes for eight hours from the snowbound train just to catch up with her!

The train sped across the country, passing Albuquerque and on to Chicago. In Chicago, Nellie was honored with a quick breakfast at the Chicago Press Club. She was the first woman to walk through its door. In Pittsburg, there was an enormous crowd on the platform, cheering their hometown heroine. Nellie's mother and a couple of friends boarded the train in Philadelphia to join her for the final triumphant ride. At 3:51 p.m. on January 25, 1890, Nellie Bly arrived in Jersey City where she had started out. She had traveled 24,899 miles in seventy-two days, six hours. and eleven minutes, a record that would remain unbroken for thirty-nine years.

Nellie did not linger in New Jersey but rushed on to New York City, where she was honored with a champagne celebration. Home at last!

Elizabeth Bisland, her competitor, also circled the globe in fewer than eighty days. She arrived back in New York four days after Nellie—to a much quieter reception.

Nellie was immediately caught up in her moment of celebrity. She completed her articles for *The World* and quickly expanded them into book form. She appeared in advertisements for Pears Soap, although her skin now had an unladylike tan. The monkey, McGinty, did not take well to apartment life and reportedly broke every dish in the kitchen. Some accounts say that Nellie donated him to the Central Park Zoo, but others dispute this.

Soon after her historic trip, Nellie had a falling out with her employers at *The World,* for reasons that have never been explained. She left her position there and went on a lecture tour, earning hefty sums of money for discussing her travels. She continued to write, often about serious issues, but she withdrew from public scrutiny, and eventually from reporting.

Her life continued with plenty of ups and downs, including marriage to a man forty-four years older than she was, a successful new career as the manufacturer of steel barrels, and being cheated of two million dollars, forcing her into years of fruitless court cases.

Later in life, needing money, Nellie returned to journalism, and to the topics that had always made her burn: corruption, child abuse, and the prejudice against women in business. She was always tenacious in going after the heart of a story, but she did not revisit the sensational impact of her youth.

When Nellie died in 1922, the obituary in *The World* pronounced her "the best reporter in America."

Well, yes. And why not?

Nellie Bly was perhaps everything that Daisy Ashford was not—an adult, a traveler, and perhaps not quite genteel.

But Daisy achieved one thing that Nellie would have liked—her novel is still in print more than one hundred and twenty years after she wrote it.

Daisy Ashford

1881–1972

"I adored writing and used to pray for bad weather, so that I need not go out but could stay in and write."

That was what the adult Daisy had to say on the subject of rain. Here is a page, spelling mistakes included, likely from an essay assigned by her governess, when she was a lot younger:

"I like a rainy day except it makes the earth wet and flabby. Nurses are always cross on wet days that you feel you could go to sleep. You feel your chest is alive and is thumping you. The best thing to do on a wet day is to drink coffee in the kitchen like I did once. Grown up people had better dance the sailors hornpipe or sew. Gentlemen had better warm thear feet and read."

 ⁓

I t was lucky for Daisy Ashford, and for her readers, that she lived in England—famous for its numerous rainy days. Daisy began her writing career before she could even form letters; her patient parents, Emma and Willie, were happy to copy down her every word. In total, she composed six novelettes, but Daisy stopped writing at the age of fourteen, not knowing that one of her books would become a bestseller still available more than one hundred years after she wrote it.

Daisy's mother had first been married to a man named Harry, and had three sons and two daughters before he died. As a widow in the 1870s, with five young children, Emma's hopes for a prosperous future were dim. She felt lucky to meet and fall in love with Willie Ashford. Willie was just as happy to suddenly have a big, boisterous household after many years of loneliness. Emma and Willie added three more daughters to the family, beginning in 1881 with Daisy, whose formal name was Margaret Mary Julia. Vera and Angie soon followed. The older boys were sent away to boarding school, but the large house in the country was busy and noisy. The girls lived a sheltered life while they were young, taking daily lessons with a governess.

As was customary for middle- and upper-class girls, Daisy and her sisters spent much of their indoor time in the schoolroom or day nursery—a different place from the night nursery where they slept. They were taught very little about geography or science or mathematics and a great deal about literature and art. Daisy's family especially prized being well-read and able to discuss music and theatre, politics and world affairs. The girls had frequent outings, and the household had many visitors.

In a time before television or radio, the family created its own amusements. They put on plays, wrote clever verses, memorized passages to recite, and read to each other aloud.

It was Willie's sister, Aunt Julia, who first began to write letters to three-year-old Daisy, and Emma who thought of answering them, using the little girl's own words and even her childish pronunciation, as in this excerpt:

> Dear Auntie,
> I'm writing a letter for dear Auntie . . . I like you so much . . . I can't be rocked now 'cos I'm 3. I go to sleep wizout rocking all by myself. . . . There was a little boy at Prior Park & some big boy knocked him down & there was a roller there right at the bottom of the hill. He's dead, dead now, a roller killed him . . .
> I've a lot of words to tell Auntie . . . You're a good woman and Father's a good gekleum,
> From
> Daydums

Already, Daisy knew enough to intrigue her reader by choosing an exciting incident to report.

According to family legend, when Daisy was four, she sneaked into her father's study and hid under the desk while he was talking with a visiting priest. After the guest had gone, Daisy emerged and told her father that she wanted to write a story about Father McSwiney. Willie kindly picked up his pen and told Daisy to begin.

"So with hands clasped behind her back, she walked up and down the room and dictated an entirely fictitious biography of four thousand words," that included an encounter with the Pope on a railway platform and many saintly deeds.

Daisy's mother, Emma, created an adaptation of "Cinderella," in rhyme, for the children to perform at one of their family gatherings. Several years later, this inspired Daisy to write a play herself, called *A Woman's Crime*. Her sister Vera designed a poster for it. Her sister Angie played the heroine. She was stabbed to death by Vera. The script has been lost, but it was apparently quite funny, despite the gruesome crime: "The butler informs the lady of the house that her daughter is lying dead upstairs: 'I will go to her at once,' she announces. 'Oh, no, madam,' the butler says. 'I will bring the body down.'"

Daisy's first book, *A Short Story of Love and Marriage*, was dictated to her father when she was eight. The following year, she was ready to write down her own words. As she scribbled away in her red-covered notebook, other creative minds were at work elsewhere in the world; during that year, 1890, the game of basketball was invented, as well as the paper clip, the zipper, and the fountain pen.

Lewis Carroll's *Alice's Adventures in Wonderland* had been published twenty-five years earlier. *The Tale of Peter Rabbit,* by Beatrix Potter, *The Jungle Book,* by Rudyard Kipling, and *Peter Pan,* by J. M. Barrie, were all yet to be written. But Daisy's masterpiece was complete, all ten thousand words! Although her spelling and punctuation were not always accurate, she had a good understanding of characters and plot. The book was called *The Young Visiters*—yes, misspelled—and holds many colorful details, beginning with the opening line: "Mr. Salteena was an elderly man of 42 and was fond of asking people to stay with him . . ." Daisy went on to tell us that "Mr. Salteena had dark short hair and mustache and wiskers which were very black and twisty . . ."

The author quickly introduced the seventeen-year-old heroine of the story, who is Mr. Salteena's ward. ("Keeping a ward" was a frequent practice in upper-middle-class Victorian England. It meant being responsible for a young person's education and introduction to society.) "Ethel Monticue had fair hair done on the top and blue eyes. She had a blue velvit frock which had grown rarther short in the arms."

By the end of the first page, Daisy deftly started the plot moving in a letter that arrives attached to a "quear shaped parcel."

> My dear Alfred,
>
> I want you to come for a stop with me so I have sent you a top hat wraped up in tishu paper inside the box. Will you wear it staying with me because it is very uncommon. Please bring one of your young ladies whichever is the prettiest in the face.
>
> I remain Yours truly,
>
> Bernard Clark

In Mr. Salteena's reply to Bernard's letter, Daisy revealed the secret longing that propels her main character through the book: "I am not quite a gentleman but you would hardly notice it but cant be helped anyhow. We will come by the 3:15 [train]."

Despite his pretense of not really caring, Mr. Salteena is driven to improve himself, partly because he has a second hidden wish—to marry Ethel. But he makes the mistake of taking her to visit Bernard Clark, where the reader sees at once what the author has in mind: "A tall man of 29 rose from the sofa. He was rarther bent in the middle with very nice long legs, fairish hair and blue eyes."

Is it love at first sight?

"Oh yes gasped Ethel blushing through her red ruge. Bernard looked at her keenly and turned a dark red. I am glad to see you he said . . ."

The Young Visiters follows the progress of the love story, alongside poor Mr. Salteena's efforts to become a gentleman, even when he recognizes Bernard's claim on Ethel's affections.

In the end, Mr. Salteena has the honor of meeting the Prince of

Wales, "nervously wishing he had got correct knickerbockers," but triumphant nonetheless.

And there is, of course, a wedding, where Ethel wears a dress of "rich satin with a humped pattern of gold on the pure white," and a veil "of pure lace with a crown of orange blossom." The banquet includes many delicacies, from "jam tarts with plenty of jam on each" to "a pig's head done up in a wondrous manner." When the wedding supper is done, "everybody got a bag of rice and sprinkled on the pair and Mr. Salteena sadly threw a white tennis shoe at them wiping his eyes the while."

Daisy's final work, *The Hangman's Daughter*, was finished at the age of fourteen. "I put so much more effort into it than any of the others," a grown-up Daisy said about this last book, which took her a year to write. "By this time I had really determined to become an authoress (an ambition which entirely left me after my school days) . . . I shall never forget my feeling of shock when I read it aloud to my brothers and they laughed at the trial scene!"

The children's manuscripts and drawings, all carefully saved by their mother, were not seen or thought of again until Emma died, thirty years later, at which point the literary treasure trove was discovered in one of her drawers.

By then, Daisy was an adult. She had married James Devlin and started a family. Knowing that her friend Margaret would see great humor in the rediscovery of her childhood opus, Daisy sent her *The Young Visiters* as an amusement while she was recovering from the flu. But Margaret was excited and passed it along until it reached the book publishing house of Chatto and Windus. Recognizing the charm of a precocious child's masterpiece, they chose to publish the book with all the errors intact.

They also invited J. M. Barrie to write the introduction. He was the famous man who had created *Peter Pan,* and he became an avid fan of Daisy Ashford. A rumor circulated that *The Young Visiters* had actually been written by him. But no, it was truly a small scribbler who had created the work that would become a play, a movie, and a continued success in the book stores, more than one hundred years later.

Daisy gave her heroine and hero a happy ending:

Bernard Clark was the happiest of our friends as he loved Ethel
to the bitter end and so did she him and they had a nice house
too . . . So now my readers we will say farewell to the characters
in this book.

Daisy Ashford's book came about because she was surrounded by loving family members, each of whom prized the written word.

Ada Blackjack wrote because she was surrounded by men making observations in scientific journals, each of them showing her that the smallest details can add up to big stories.

Ada Blackjack

1898–1983

One day just after I had cleaned my second seal I heard a noise like a dog . . . and I looked out the door and about fifteen feet from the tent was a big bear and a young one. I was very scared but I took my rifle and thought I would take a chance. I knew if I just hit them in the foot or some place where it would only injure them a little they would come after me, so I fired over their heads . . .

Ada Blackjack was more afraid of polar bears than anything else—including being alone on a remote island north of Russian Siberia with a dead man in the next tent. She had never held a rifle before she went north, but she learned to use one when her survival depended on it.

Ada is sometimes referred to as the "Heroine of Wrangel Island," although she certainly did not set out to do anything heroic. She was hired, under shady pretenses, to be the seamstress on a secret expedition in the Arctic. With four men, seven sled dogs, and one kitten, she traveled to desolate, windswept Wrangel. Two years later, a rescue ship found Ada alone, all her companions dead or disappeared. Despite the harrowing adventure, and her lack of formal education, Ada kept a journal for the last several months of her ordeal, telling her side of the story.

Ada Delutuk, an Inupiat Eskimo, was born in 1898, the same year that gold was discovered in her home state of Alaska, and the same year that Robert Peary set out on his second expedition to the Arctic pole. She grew up in the tiny settlement of Spruce Creek. (When Ada was alive, the word used for her people was Eskimo, so that is what will be used here.)

When she was sixteen, Ada married a man named Jack Blackjack. She had three babies with him, but only one, a son named Bennett, lived past infancy. Ada's marriage ended after six years, leaving her with no support and a sick little boy. Bennett had tuberculosis and needed a doctor's care. But doctors cost money, and Ada had none. She placed her son in an orphanage, where he could be cared for while she found herself a job.

Eventually, Ada found work as a housecleaner, earning barely enough to pay for her own expenses. She was on her way home one evening, feeling blue after a long day, when she was stopped by the local police chief, who was an acquaintance. He informed her that Eskimos were being recruited for an expedition to the north. He knew that Ada's superior abilities as a seamstress would be an important qualification.

Staying warm and dry in the Arctic was a matter of life and death; the success of any mission to the far north relied on having animal skin clothing properly constructed and repaired to protect against bitterly cold winds and icy waters. The seams were carefully rolled and stitched to remain watertight. The sewing needle was the most essential tool used by the Eskimo people.

Ada didn't like the idea of being so far away from her son, but they were promising what seemed like a vast amount of money: fifty dollars a month! There would be other Eskimos on the trip, she was told. The men would hunt to provide food for the scientists, the women would sew the necessary fur garments, and they'd all come home rich.

The expedition was the idea of a man named Vilhjalmur Stefansson, a dashing Canadian of Icelandic heritage. He was an ethnologist as well as an explorer, meaning that he studied the culture and customs of various ethnic groups. He had lived in the Arctic for two years, learning to hunt and live as the northern natives did, and he'd written and published a book called *My Life With the Eskimos*.

In 1910, Stefansson discovered a previously unknown tribe of fair-haired Eskimos, who still used primitive tools. He conjectured that they were of Viking descent, though that idea has since been disproved. He believed passionately that the Arctic was not a bleak wasteland, but that it could be settled by white men, particularly those willing to live off the land, as the natives did.

Stefansson's public reputation was shaky, however, and with good reason. He had been commander of an earlier Arctic expedition sponsored by the Canadian government, and had abandoned his ship when it became trapped by ice. The ship eventually was crushed and sank. The men on it were lost, while Stefansson and two others proceeded by sledge across the frozen oceans, surviving for ninety six days on what he could shoot with his rifle.

Stefansson was convinced—correctly, as it turned out—that the North Pole lay in the center of an undocumented continent. But his dream was not to pursue the location of the pole. He wanted to secretly claim land—already Russian territory—for Canada and the British Empire. His objective was a place called Wrangel Island.

Ada went to visit a shaman, who confirmed that she would go to the island, but that "death and danger" waited there. Despite this warning, Ada accepted the job. Her need for money to look after Bennett outweighed the stomach-churning worry.

She was given an allowance to buy supplies: needles, sinew, thread, and thimbles, which were used to protect the fingers when stitching through heavy material like animal hides. She also bought towels and handkerchiefs, and one precious Eversharp pencil. In 1921, Eversharp pencils were a recent invention; the first mass-produced mechanical pencils, they featured a mechanism that propelled a strand of lead into the writing shaft, and so they never had to be sharpened. They were so popular that the company was manufacturing 35,000 every day. Ada treasured hers above almost any other possession.

Stefansson was not leading the venture this time. Between dates on a successful lecture tour, he would live in New York. He had hired four young men to represent his interests in the Arctic: Lorne Knight and Fred Maurer, who had been with him on a previous excursion; Milton Galle, from Texas; and Allan Crawford, a fellow Canadian, designated leader so that he could be the official claimant of Wrangel Island, under Stefansson's direction.

The men met Ada in Nome, Alaska, in September of 1921, when they arrived on the boat *Victoria*. The steward had presented them with a good luck kitten, soon named Vic. Their destination was undisclosed, because Stefansson wanted the small colony in place before word of his intentions leaked out. The newspaper reporters who followed them about assumed they knew a secret source of gold, left over from the gold rush years before.

The other Eskimos who had been hired did not show up for departure. Ada was assured that an Eskimo family would join the party at the next stop. Reluctantly, she boarded the *Silver Wave*, bound for the unknown.

In East Cape, Siberia, the Russian governor was suspicious about the purpose of this mission, but laughed when he heard the destination. Why would anyone go there?

He warned them to respect the fact that Wrangel Island was Russian territory. Far more worrisome to Ada was that no local Eskimo was willing to come along. Despite her dismay, Ada thought about the money and allowed herself to be talked into going.

On September 16, 1921, after a stormy crossing, the *Silver Wave* deposited five people, eight animals, and small mountains of equipment on a bleak and windy beach. While Ada watched the parting ship with a mournful heart, the four men unfurled the British flag and claimed the island on behalf of King George V.

The plan was to stay on Wrangel Island for two years, but they brought with them supplies for only the first six months of winter. Part of the experiment was to "live off the land," hunting and fishing for food as the Eskimos did. However, they had failed to purchase one item essential for survival: the *umiak*, or small hunting kayak that was used for skimming through icy waters in pursuit of seals or walrus.

The first few days on site were spent building tents and setting up camp. Lorne Knight and Fred Mauer had been in the north before, but Crawford and Galle were having their first adventure in the Arctic. As for Ada, her biographer wrote that "she was barely five feet tall, unskilled, timid, and completely ignorant of the world outside Nome, Alaska. She

was deathly afraid of guns and of polar bears. She knew nothing about hunting, trapping, living off the land, or even building an igloo."

The early days of adjustment were tough. The men did not warm up to Ada, and they recorded that Ada acted a bit crazily with homesickness and panic. She developed a big crush on Allen Crawford, whose green eyes could set her mooning, causing the men to ridicule her. She seems to have suffered from something called "Arctic hysteria," a temporary mental illness that causes the victim to be in a slump, to cry frequently, to run away, and to behave erratically. After many days and punishments from the men, Ada's condition subsided. She resolved to pull her weight, and she became industrious and more congenial. The men began to trust her, creating the sense of a team.

As fall became winter, the colonists settled into a routine. The men each had scientific studies to make, along with the basic requirements of survival that kept them steadily occupied. Their favorite dog, Snowball, died in November, and a second one died a short while later.

There were several close calls with polar bears, who were sometimes bold enough to sniff their way right into the tent. Lorne Knight wrote in his diary that one time, "the fellows started to throw things; first the firewood, and then the pots and pans, and finally dishes. Of course, the bear was hit several times, but he was determined to come in. His old snoot was working from side to side and the digestive juices were dropping from the end of his tongue. I guess he was hungry." That particular bear finally fled—too quickly to be shot for supper.

The long, dark weeks of winter arrived, with sixty-one days of "night" between November and January, when it was light for only about an hour out of twenty-four. The group was not prepared for the ordeal ahead. None of them had medical know-how, and so minor problems became aggravated without the proper attention. Lorne Knight made a disastrous exploratory trek into the wilderness during the spring of 1922, and nearly died when he had to swim across the frigid Skeleton River to get back to camp.

As summer approached, they looked forward to the arrival of the promised ship, carrying a stock of food, ammunition, and materials.

There was a narrow access period during the summer months when a ship could pass through the ice-choked Chukchi Sea. Ada, especially, resolved to take the opportunity to escape from Wrangel Island, and return to her mother and Bennett.

Unbeknownst to the waiting group, Stefansson's efforts had been held up by a lack of funds, and perhaps an attitude that renewed provisions were not crucial. Stefansson, the optimistic Arctic-lover, was fond of saying things like, "I think that anyone with good eyesight and a rifle can live anywhere in the Polar Regions indefinitely."

Relief was sent too late. Captain Bernard, on board the *Teddy Bear*, tried valiantly to cut through the frozen waters north of Siberia, but "the report was grim—nothing but a solid wall of ice across the horizon in the direction of Wrangel Island." Heartsick, he was forced to turn back.

"The boys expected a boat up until the last of October," said Ada. "Around about November they knew the boat wouldn't come."

Stefansson was not particularly worried that he'd left arrangements for relief too late and that "his" expedition was stranded for at least a year past their expectations. "This means merely that the men on the island are cut off from communication for a year," Stefansson wrote to Milton Galle's mother. "They are just as safe on their island as Robinson Crusoe was on his—a little more so because there are no cannibals in that vicinity." His overconfidence—some would say negligence—would prove to be fatal.

The colonists on Wrangel Island were eating their way through the pieces of a walrus, even the flippers, which were difficult chewing. Slowly came the dismal realization that the ice had closed in, making the arrival of a relief ship impossible. They were sentenced to a second miserable winter.

"At Christmas time we had some salt seal meat and some hard bread and tea for our Christmas dinner," Ada said later. "I wondered where I would be if I lived until next Christmas." Though wildlife had seemed abundant when they'd first arrived, it became dramatically scarcer and had not reappeared in the spring as anticipated, meaning they'd not been able to dry and salt much reserve food.

In desperation, in January of 1923, Knight and Crawford set out with the five remaining dogs, intending to walk across the ice to Siberia. If all went well, it would take sixty or seventy days to reach civilization, and as many again to return with fresh supplies. They left farewell letters to their families in camp, in case some disaster prevented their return. Only a week later they were back. January was the deadliest month in the north, dark for about twenty hours each day. They had been thwarted by a blinding blizzard, and Knight's weakening health had quickly worsened when faced with the grueling physical demands of hiking in the Arctic.

They quickly decided that Knight should remain in camp with Ada, and the other three men would make the trek instead. It was their only hope. While preparations were made that week, they measured temperatures as cold as fifty-six degrees below zero Fahrenheit.

On January 28, Crawford, Mauer, and Galle left for Siberia. They took their diaries but Galle left his typewriter, telling Ada firmly not to touch it in his absence. Again, each wrote a farewell letter to his family. They took all the dogs, leaving Vic the cat with Ada and Knight.

Those three men and the dogs were never seen again.

Ada "made a calendar out of typewriting paper cut into small pieces," to help keep track of the passing days. She wrote a note in the margin saying: "Why Galle leave?" He had been a cheerful companion, the one who behaved most like a friend to Ada. His departure must have left a real hole, making Ada entirely responsible for the ailing Knight and for the upkeep of the camp.

In February, Ada found Knight collapsed in the snow and had to drag him to his bed in the tent. He finally confessed that he suspected his condition was due to scurvy. This terrible disease attacks when a person is on a limited diet and not getting the right nutrients from his food, particularly the vitamin C in fruits and vegetables. Using the encyclopedia on the expedition bookshelf, Knight began an obsessive tracking of his symptoms and what might lie ahead. He continued to write in his journal every day, and many of the available details of these weeks are thanks to his record.

Ada's life back in Nome had not involved setting traps or shooting.

She was deathly afraid of the "boam" (boom) that guns made, but soon her survival would depend on overcoming this fear.

Maurer left Ada with a map of his trap lines, so that she would know where to go each day to check for animals and to reset the traps. In the beginning, she didn't understand how the traps worked, but after a few failures and an empty stomach, she triumphantly caught her first fox. Knight gave her a lesson in shooting the rifle, but her efforts were not impressive and Knight sneered at her.

Apart from the time that Ada spent doing the work she'd accomplished before with the help of four men, there were a few hours of each day that she and Knight now spent confined together. They realized that it made the best sense to heat only one space, so they were sharing a tent about the size of a small, low garage, with a wood-burning stove, two cots, all their food, and other supplies.

They did not have much to talk about. Knight wrote in his journal that, as a conversationalist, "she's bunk." But they soon had a routine of telling each other fairy and folk tales. Ada loved to hear Knight's version of "Jack and the Beanstalk." Her favorite story to tell was an Eskimo legend called "The Lady in the Moon," about a young girl on a quest who takes the wrong fork in the road and comes home transformed into an old woman, with no kin left to greet her.

Knight had brought his family Bible on the expedition. Ada, already a Christian believer, pored over the colored plates and beautiful type for hours, touching the pictures with her fingers, becoming more devout.

In the middle of March, Ada began to write a journal. Each of the men had devotedly kept a log while they were on Wrangel Island, documenting scientific and personal observations, but Ada was not used to expressing herself on paper. Although her English was not perfect and she made plenty of spelling mistakes, her handwriting was clear and round, like that of a schoolteacher. Her actual, uncorrected words are reproduced here, to share the sense of her "voice." The early entries were mostly a trapping log and a recitation of her daily chores, with occasional news of other kinds, but eventually Ada warmed up to the idea of writing more about her worries and her small triumphs.

The diary begins:

Made in March 14th, 1923. The frist fox I caught was in feb. 21st
and then second March 3 and 4th, 5th, that makes 4 white foxes . . .

On March 12 she trapped three foxes in one day. She made fox soup,
served with raw seagull eggs. Because of his illness, Knight's teeth were
so loose in his gums that he could no longer chew and could hardly even
swallow.

March 16th. I have not feeling well for three day frist I was head-
ach and then I had stumpick trouble and today I feel much
better. I was over to the traps with no fox or fresh tracks. And
last night knight told me I can keep the bible he said he give
them to me, very nice day so far.

The style of Ada's writing is not literary, the content is often repeti-
tive and mundane, but the fact that it exists at all is as miraculous as anything she might have prayed for while thumbing through Lorne Knight's
family Bible.

26th
. . . I haul one load of sled and saw four cuts of log and chop
wood, and we look at knights legs my! They are skinny and they
has no more blue spots like they use to be.

During the month of March, Ada managed to trap thirteen foxes,
including one that had dragged a trap away on its foot a few days before,
and returned to be trapped again. "It has caught trap by trap that funny,"
she wrote.

Over the next few days, Ada suffered from an ailment that caused
her eyelids and face to swell badly, leaving her unable to do the chores.
She was clearly worried because on April 2 she wrote instructions, "If
anything happen to me and my death is known . . ." She had made a

black strap for Bennett's school bag and asked that it be sent to him, "for my only son. I wish if you please take everything to Bennett that is belong to me. I don't know how much I would be glad to get home to folks."

Within a few days she was back to work, with her eyes much better. The main concern each day was whether the wind was blowing too hard for her to leave the tent, and whether or not the traps held a fox or two. In between checking the traps, she sewed, cut wood, melted snow for their water supply, and prepared what little food they had.

On April 21 they were still surrounded by ice and could not hope to sight a relief ship until June, when the ice began to break up. Knight must have been frustrated nearly beyond endurance, knowing what little hope he had of survival. Ada chopped wood that day but did not get out to the traps. "And when I come in and build the fire knight started to cruel with me . . ."

She continued with her longest entry in the diary, obviously needing to vent her sadness. Knight had said terrible things to her; he'd applauded Ada's husband for being mean, saying that she deserved it, he'd claimed that Ada did nothing to help Knight, "And he menitions my children and saying no wonder your children die you never take good care of them. He just tear me into pieces when he menition my children that I lost. This is the wosest life I ever live in the world . . ."

The possibility of death was clearly on Ada's mind. Again she wrote her "last wishes":

If I be known dead, I want my sister Rita to take Bennett my son for her own son and look after everythings for Bennett she is the only one that I wish she take my son don't let his father Black Jack take him, if Rita my sister live. Then I be clear.
Ada B. Jack.

The following day, she wrote: "Apr. 22. I didn't go out today because I was just chock with cry." Deeply hurt by the terrible scene with Knight, Ada spent much of the next few days sleeping and reading the Bible.

Apr. 29th. Still blowing I didn't go out. And knight said he was pretty sick and I didn't say nothing because I have nothing to say and he got mad and he through a book at me . . . And I didn't say nothing to him and before I went in my sleeping bag I fell his water cup and went to bed.

May 3 provides the first sign that spring might come: "I was out to chop wood today and I saw snow bird. Oh my how I am glad to see some snow birds come . . ."

Knight was failing. "He was so weak that I had to hold his head to give him a drink of water. I made a canvas bag and filled this bag with hot sand to keep his feet warm, every morning and night for two months I heated this sand and put it to his feet."

May 10, 1923, was Ada's twenty-fifth birthday, but she didn't mention that in her diary. She later said that she awoke to the sound of dripping and thought it was rain, or even ice thawing from the warmth of spring. But it was the sound of Knight's nose bleeding. "He had a one-pound tea tin half full of blood," and "his face was just blue."

"I think he was pretty near die this morning," she wrote. On May 12, she said, "I fry one biscuit for knight that's all he eat for 9 days he don't look like he is going to live very long . . ."

The traps were empty, day after day. Knight got weaker and sicker. Ada tended to him and stitched away, making herself warm clothes, producing a "blanked coat" and a "clothe parky." She made herself do target practice, knowing their lives depended on it. She saw more birds every day, but flying birds are tricky targets and she had only occasional luck. On June 7, she spotted a "see gall"—a seagull—"and I took a shot at him and I got him dead shot. Oh my! It good and I eat no meat for long time . . ."

On June 8, Ada had another nursing duty for Knight, the unpleasant task of cutting a hole through his sleeping bag so that he could use a bedpan. She also saw fresh polar bear tracks on the beach near the camp.

On June 10, Ada needed a new journal, but what could she use for paper? Knight suggested a photographic supply order book that sat empty with their supplies. So she began a second volume, clearly restating on the first page that she was appointing her sister, Rita, as guardian of Bennett, preferred over Black Jack, his father: "I know she love Bennett just as much as I do I dare not my son to have stepmother. If you please let this know to the Judge." She also gave directions as to where her pay from the expedition should go—to her mother, Mrs. Ototook, and to Rita to care for Bennett. She followed the official request with her signature, and the plaintive, "I just write noted in case Polar bear tear me down . . ."

The report on her companion that day is this: "knight is very sick he hardly talk and he is skinny my he nothing but skin and bone he lay in his sleeping bag for four month he pretty near die 10th of May and 12th..."

But there they both were, well into June. Knight was still alive, surely thanks to Ada's care. She suffered from snow blindness that week, but still, "I found one see gall egg and that one geese I got she has one egg and two smale ones knight eat some egg he cann't eat meat."

She couldn't go out for several days because of the soreness of her eyes. Then she started practicing her shooting again, determined to bring in some birds.

> June 17. I wash my clothes today and I shot once to a Idars [eider duck]. and this evening I made a target and shot two times with the rifle. and I took my target in and show it to knight and he said its pretty good shooting and I saw a creek flowing to the harbar.

That entry tells us two important things: Knight had paid her the highest compliment he could—to congratulate her on good shooting. And the creek actually *flowing* meant that the ice was slowly breaking up.

> June 21 . . . knight is getting very bad he looks like he is going to die.

Ada felt the situation was dire enough that she broke her promise to Milton Galle and used his typewriter:

Dear Galle, I didn't know I will have very important writing to do. You will forgive me wouldn't you . . . Mr. Knight he hardly know what he's talking about I guess he is going die he looks pretty bad . . . Yours truly Mrs. Ada B. Jack

Knight died that night. Her next handwritten entry reads: "June 22. I move to the other tent today and I was my dishes and getting some wood."

Ada did not announce Knight's death in her diary because she made an official declaration using the typewriter:

Wrangel Island
June 23rd, 1923
The daid of Mr. Knights death. He died on June 23rd I don't know what time he die though Anyway I write the daid, Just to let Mr. Stefansson know what month he died and what daid of the month. writen by Mrs Ada B. Jack

Later, Ada said, "I had hard time when he was dying. I never will forget that all my life. I was crying while he was living. I try my best to save his life but I can't quite save him."

She was now alone—except for Vic the cat—in the frozen waste-land, at least sixty days' walk from the nearest settlement, but in which direction? Ada had no idea. All her faith had to focus on a ship making its way through the ice. The ground was too hard to bury Knight. She left him lying inside his tent in his sleeping bag. She stacked boxes around him to discourage animals and to mask the smell of his body decaying. Knight had asked her to preserve his journal, which she now protected with his camera in a box under a tarp.

Ada had no choice but to keep hunting and chopping wood and learning new tricks of survival. She even tried to make a visual record of her new solitude: "I took pictures of this tent and myself I don't know how I work the camra." And later, "June 25. I was taking walk over to little Island and I found three see gall eggs in one nest. And I cook them for my lunch I take tea and saccharine I had a nice picknick all by myself."

On June 27, "I saw a seal and I went after it and got it with one shot . . . That's a frist seal I ever got in my life."

The next day she heard a funny noise, and when she looked out through the door, she:

> . . . saw Polar bear and one cub. I was very afraid so I took a shot over them see if they would go so they went away and they were looking back and I shot five times and they run away.
>
> July 1st. I stay home today and I fix the shovel handle that I brack this spring and I saw Polar bear out on the ice and this evening I went to the end of the sand spit shot a eidar duck I shot him right in the head thank God keep me a live till now.

The migration of seals across Ada's beach continued to provide food and target practice, though a polar bear and cub staged a raid and stole one whole freshly killed seal. She had moments of summer, "all day very nice and sunshines," but she never forgot that she might be there through bad weather again. She steadily dried food, knitted mittens, repaired her boots, and fixed up the structure of her tent, assembling an observation platform on stilts to improve her view. Her sewing began to get fancier; she mentions beading and wolf-fur trim, chosen for hoods because it did not freeze when breathed on.

In mid-July, Ada made herself a canvas boat, and although she had no experience in boat-building:

> . . . it works all right this afternoon I got three old sqaws [female seals] and I use the boat I made.
>
> July 19. . . . the beach got open water . . .

On July 24, she heard walrus, and the next night, "oh yes I dreamed I was singing three cheer for the red white and blue."

Two days later:

I clean seal flappers and put them away in case ship comes so I
can take them home and eat them with my sisters . . .
    July 30. . . . the ice is broken to piece quite many open leads.

Early in August, her canvas boat floated away, but "I made another
canves boat, better this time." She proudly made oars, too!
    Ada sighted polar bears—or their tracks—close to camp nearly every
day, but her main focus was how the ice was breaking up on the water.
One morning, she found that the lard can where she'd been storing her
seal blubber had been emptied by a polar bear in the night. She worked
hard on knitting a seal net to help her hunting. She also unraveled a sock
from the dwindling supplies, to give her wool to knit new gloves.

Aug. 20. I finished my knitted gloves today and I open last biscuit box. The ice is over little below horizon. I thank the lord
Jesus and his father.

That is the final entry in the diary. She awoke the next morning
and heard a sound that she first assumed was a walrus. But soon it got
louder. Ada scrambled to her lookout and peered through the fog with
her binoculars.
    A ship.

The Eskimos on the deck of the *Donaldson* cheered. They could see a
forlorn figure through the fog and knew they were in time to save someone. The greeting was emotional. The skipper, Harold Noice, gathered
a weeping Ada into his arms and carried her back to the ship.
    When she had warmed up and recovered a little, Noice and Ada re-
turned to shore to collect the only other survivor, Vic the cat, as well as
Ada's possessions and all the papers belonging to the men. The crew dug
a grave for Knight and held a ceremony. Ada said good-bye to the island
where she had lived for almost two years.

Noice encouraged Ada to write down her story while on board the boat, to the best of her recollection.

Although he later cast suspicion on Ada's character, Noice, for now, was her savior. After their return, unexplained motives compelled Noice to perform several confusing acts: he tampered with Knight's diary, he withheld documents from the grieving families, and he suggested that Ada had allowed Knight to die, or worse, had killed him.

Ada was able to convince Knight's family of the truth and she was not formally accused. But life was never easy for her. She married a man named Johnson and had another son, Billy, but the second marriage also ended unhappily. Because she was poor and not well, Ada was obliged to put Billy and Bennett into a children's residence for nine years. When she finally scraped together enough money, she reclaimed the two boys and worked herding reindeer. She relied on her Wrangel Island skills to feed the children by hunting and trapping. Billy eventually moved away, but Bennett continued to live with his mother.

Ada avoided publicity as much as possible. She died in May 1983, just after her eighty-fifth birthday.

Wrangel Island is now a Russian wildlife refuge, with a small scientific community and a Chukchi Inuit settlement. The animals living there are mostly the polar bears that Ada feared so much, as well as walrus and reindeer. There is still a feeling of mystery about the place because it is nearly always icebound and often drenched in a thick fog.

Allan Crawford was the young, green-eyed Canadian who disappeared on his journey across the ice to find help. During the difficult time of making decisions about her son's papers, his mother received a letter from a friend. That letter contained this sentence: "Real history is made up from the documents that were not meant to be published."

The story of Ada Blackjack is profound proof of that fact.

Ada Blackjack went to the Arctic to help support her young son, but she missed him terribly throughout her ordeal.

Dang Thuy Tram, separated from all familiar loved ones in wartime, also thought and wrote about her family every day that she was away.

Dr. Dang Thuy Tram

1943—1970

5 November 1969

At this moment, how many families are homeless? Where do their gaunt children live?

Oh! Cruel American bandits, your crimes are piling up like a mountain. As long as I live, I vow to fight until my last drop of blood . . .

&

S adly, "as long as I live" turned out to be not long at all. Dang Thuy Tram was twenty-seven years old when she wrote those words seven months before she died—shot in the head with an American bullet.

Thuy was eleven in 1954 when her homeland of Vietnam was divided into two separate countries, North and South, at war with each other. She was twenty-two, and studying to become a doctor, when the United States became involved in the conflict, supporting South Vietnam's fight against the Communist North, where Thuy lived.

Two years later, now officially Dr. Dang, Thuy set off from the capital city of Hanoi to a remote jungle clinic in Duc Pho, in the province of Quong Ngai, smack in the middle of the war zone. Shortly before her arrival, the hospital building had been bombed and replaced by a primitive temporary facility.

The Vietnamese people have a high regard for poetic expression, and, like many young women embarking on a new venture, Thuy wrote frequently and passionately in her journal. Her entries show how she missed her family, friends, and home, and record her harrowing experience as a military doctor.

Thuy was the eldest of four sisters and a brother. Her father was a surgeon, and her mother was an expert in the use of medicinal plants and a lecturer at the Hanoi School of Pharmacology. Being a healer was clearly in Thuy's blood. Thuy's childhood, before the war began, was in a loving home, full of books, music, and fresh flowers. She took violin lessons and studied hard at school.

Thuy often cared for her younger siblings while her parents were absent or working. This included cooking "fun stuff from eggplants and shaddocks," according to her sister, Hien, who also remembers "singing and making dramas. We used a bed as the boat, and the mat as the river."

Hard times forced their parents to be away for a year, taking two of the sisters while they looked for work, and leaving Thuy, in her last year of high school, to care for little Hien. A severe lack of money meant that the sisters "usually had to hunt for food on a meal-to-meal basis. . . . We took some fibers of breadfruit and placed them at the pond's bank and the morning after there would be snails stuck to them. Indeed we had a new source of nutrition." Catching crabs was another skill that yielded suppers, sometimes enough to share with neighbors. The resourcefulness that Thuy displayed while caring for her sister during those difficult months was excellent preparation for coping with the hunger and deprivation she would later face.

The young Thuy we meet through her private record is earnest and emotional, deeply attached to her friends. But a frightening and deadly war was a daily threat to her hope and strong spirit. As a new doctor, she repaired grisly injuries and gave comfort to dying boys who, like her, were far away from their homes and families.

By the time Thuy began the second volume of her diary (the first volume was lost) in April of 1968, there were half a million American soldiers in her country. Terrible news had arrived one month earlier from a neighboring village called Son My, where American troops had killed 504 villagers—women, children, and old men, who'd had no way to defend themselves. The North Vietnamese people felt immense sorrow and renewed fury after this event, which became known as the My Lai Massacre, named for the hamlets of the village of Son My. Although Thuy does not refer directly to the horror of My Lai, the intensity of her writing is more understandable set against the background of this tragedy.

The persistent threads in Thuy's writing are her affection and longing for her family, her belief in the ideals of her Communist country, her regret about a friendship with a man she called "M," and devotion to her patients.

The diary begins simply:

April 8, 1968: Operated on one case of appendicitis with inadequate anesthesia. I had only a few meager vials of Novocain to give the soldier but never groaned once. . . . He even smiled, to encourage me. . . . I was very sorry to find an infection in his abdomen. . . . I wanted to say, 'If I cannot even heal people like you, this sorrow will not fade from my medical career."

A few days later, Thuy heard about the death of a friend named Huong.

22 April 1968
. . . Huong died? The news stuns me like a nightmare. One comrade falls down today, another tomorrow. Will these pains ever end? Heaps of flesh and bones keep piling up into a mountain of hatred rising ever taller in our hearts. When? When and when comrades? When can we chase the entire bloodthirsty mob from our motherland?

Much of the forest in the region of the clinic was like a dense hedge as high as a house, with trails like tunnels cut through it. Soldiers, as well as the medical facility itself, were camouflaged, and not visible from the helicopters droning overheard. Thuy often mentioned the jungle or the weather to set the mood or reflect her feelings, as in these excerpts:

July comes again to our jungle, with its southern wind bothering the trees . . .

The cold wind whistling through the roadside trees, I remembered shivering slightly as I passed a tree whose trunk was forked cleanly into two branches.

Thuy observed and vividly described her small patch of the war. She wrote about the troops who passed through the clinic, her surgical patients, and her fellow medical teammates. She occasionally had to walk many miles to treat soldiers on the "battlefield" in odd corners of the oppressive surrounding jungle, all the while evading the enemy. That often meant sleeping in underground shelters. She passed one night standing up to her chest in water.

17 May 1968
The war goes on, death falls among us daily, like the flip of a hand. Just last night, Thin and Son were chatting with us. Thin asked Le to buy fabric for a shirt. Tonight they are two lifeless bodies within the earth of Duc Pho—this place where they had just set foot for the first time. Death takes us so easily; there is no way to prevent the losses. What sadness!

4 June 1968
Rain falls without respite. Rain deepens my sadness, its chill making me yearn for the warmth of a family reunion. If only I had wings to fly back to our beautiful house on Lo Duc Street, to eat with Dad, Mom, and my siblings, one simple meal with watercress and one night's sleep under the old cotton blanket.

By July 1968, Thuy had been assigned chief physician of her little hospital. "I alone am responsible for managing the clinic, treating the injured, teaching the class. More than ever I feel I am giving all my strength and skills to the revolution . . ."

Month drags after month, with each day bringing danger or heartbreaking news. Thuy recorded the troubles and deaths of many friends, usually addressing them as "Brother" or "Sister" in the Communist tradition of an extended family.

28 July
Brother Kha is captured! . . . Your handwriting is still imprinted clearly on the patient record. Where are you today, in chains or in a torture chamber? . . . Will I ever see you again? Your rucksack is still here; I feel a stab of pain in my heart whenever I see it.

4 August
. . . Sister Hai has brought sad news: Brother Dung died, captured and killed on site. What agony! Must I keep filling my small diary with pages of blood?

Throughout her trials as a doctor and friend, Thuy also worked hard toward becoming a member of what she called "the Party," an abbreviation for the Communist Party. This was not an automatic privilege, but one that involved high standards of behavior and displays of loyalty. Finally:

27 September, 1968
I've been admitted to the Party.
My clearest feeling today is that I must struggle to deserve the title of "communist."

Months of routine turned into years of relentless worry and peril. Thuy's experience in emergency surgeries gave her more confidence but was never a guarantee against the alarming variety of injuries that she dealt with.

25 August 1969
Sister Thu Huong, who is the village nurse, and her son were wounded in the raid this morning. Her chubby baby, as cute as

a European toddler, has two pieces of shrapnel in his lung near the heart. I don't know if he will survive.

(Happily, a footnote in the published diary tells us that this baby was saved.)

26 November 1969 [Thuy's 28th birthday]
Another year of living, another year of fire and smoke on this dangerous battlefield . . .

As American attacks got closer and more deadly, Thuy and her colleagues were forced to move around, sometimes carrying their patients on their backs, hiding whenever possible and always afraid.

On June 2, 1970, a bomb hit the clinic directly. Five people were killed. A second strike came on June 12, seeming to confirm that there must be an inside informant. The next day everyone left except Thuy, three female medics, and five men too seriously wounded to be moved.

By June 20, their supplies were utterly depleted. Thuy was in agony over whether or not to abandon the injured patients if the Americans arrived before help from her own countrymen.

20 June, 1970
Today there is only enough rice left for an evening meal. We cannot sit and watch the wounded soldiers go hungry. But if one of us goes out, there is no guarantee that she will be safe or that she can come back. There are too many dangers on the road. . . . No, I am no longer a child. I have grown up. I have passed trials of peril, but somehow, at this moment, I yearn deeply for Mom's caring hand. Even the hand of a dear one or that of an acquaintance would be enough.

Come to me, squeeze my hand, know my loneliness, and give me the love, the strength to prevail on the perilous road before me.

The diary ends there.

Thuy died two days later, on June 22, 1970, as the result of a bullet shot through her forehead. Her body was discovered on a forest path, next to a member of the North Vietnamese Army and two other people. Although the diary does not tell us, the clinic had been resupplied just before her death, and the injured men Thuy had stayed to protect had been safely evacuated.

How did Thuy's private journal become a public document that anyone can read?

There are two existing volumes of Thuy's diary: one was found by the U.S. Army in a backpack lost during one of Thuy's treks into hiding. It was later matched with the other volume, discovered after her death when the hospital was cleaned out by the American soldiers who occupied the region at that stage in the war. A young man named Fred Whitehurst had the job of sorting through papers to decide what was important from a military viewpoint. Assisting Fred, as he tossed things into a fire, was his interpreter, Sergeant Nguyen Trung Hieu, a man who spoke both English and Vietnamese. Hieu began to read the pages in a small notebook. Fred still remembers that Hieu was standing behind his left shoulder when he said, "Don't burn this one, Fred. There is fire in it already."

Against a rule of the United States Army that forbade scavenging for souvenirs, Fred held onto his prize, "a collection of pages sewn together with a cardboard cover, no bigger than a pack of cigarettes." During the next few evenings, Hieu read the poetic words aloud to Fred, who found himself enchanted by the young woman who had written them.

Fred mailed the diaries home to his father in the United States, knowing that "what I was doing could send me to jail." When he returned himself—just twenty-four years old, after three grueling years in Vietnam—he placed the precious books in the hands of a lawyer friend. Fred could not read the words himself, but he certainly wondered about the author and what might have happened to her family during the war. With sadness and remorse, he suspected that they had likely been killed by American bombs.

Nearly thirty-five years later, Fred shared the diary with his brother, Rob, who had married a Vietnamese woman and could speak and read Thuy's language. Rob was quickly hooked. He translated and copied the pages, while the brothers dreamed of returning them to the author's family.

Eventually, the Whitehursts entrusted a copy of the diary to Ted Engelman, a photographer who often traveled to Vietnam. Thuy's father and brother had died, but Ted was successful in finding her three sisters and her mother, then eighty-one years old. Seeing Thuy's handwriting, Dang Ngoc Tram said, "I felt as if my daughter was here, standing right in front of me."

In the summer of 2005, Fred and Rob Whitehurst traveled to Hanoi, shortly after the diary's publication in Vietnam. They were eager, but nervous, to meet Thuy's family. News of their mission attracted journalists and government officials, adding to the excitement over the book.

Thuy's mother and sisters gratefully welcomed Fred Whitehurst into their family, and he is now addressed by them as Brother Fred. Although Thuy cursed the American enemies, it was one of them who salvaged her diary, and made her feelings known to the world. Thuy's diary has now sold nearly half a million copies in Vietnam. It is also available in an English translation, which is the version this profile is based on.

Perhaps more importantly, Thuy's mother was able to revive her long-lost child, thanks to the gift of written words.

Absence is often the reason that words are written or exchanged, to make a connection.

Dang Thuy Tram wrote letters from the war zone, sharing details of daily life, trying to color in the unknown for the family she would never see again. Her diary—and the spirit within it—brought her mother comfort after a lapse of more than thirty years, connecting through time.

Doris Pilkington Garimara was lucky to be reunited with her mother after a separation of decades, though her words were written later, when she finally learned her own history. And Doris's story is inextricably connected to that of Margaret Catchpole from centuries earlier, when rabbits were also immigrants to the land called New South Wales.

Doris Pilkington Garimara

1937–

One day in a clearing close to the fence, the girls spied an emu and a family of six tiny black and white striped chicks strolling along behind him. While Daisy stood perfectly still behind some trees, Molly and Gracie chased and captured a chick each. The old man emu turned on them but gave up when he remembered that the other four chicks were unprotected.

The three girls waited in the seclusion of the small acacia bushes to see if anyone would come to investigate the commotion, but no one appeared, so they plucked and cooked the emu chicks for supper, accompanied by damper and washed down with black bitter tea; there was no sugar left.

This excerpt is from a book called *The Rabbit-Proof Fence*, written by Doris Pilkington. Daisy and Gracie were Doris's aunts. The girl named Molly grew up to be Doris's mother. Long before that happened, the three cousins had an escapade they would always remember. Doris later heard the story from her aunt and wrote it down. Another book, *Under the Wintamarra Tree*, tells about her own unusual and harrowing youth.

"I began writing on a typewriter," Doris said. "I had to teach myself with two fingers." Family stories are often the first place a writer looks for inspiration, but few writers have material to match Doris's.

Doris's family lived in Australia, members of the Mardu group of aboriginal people who have inhabited the "bush" in the Pilbara region for centuries.

In 1788, long before Doris's story begins, the first white people settled in Australia—seven boatloads of convicts transported from England, watched over by red-coated soldiers. Although the English were delighted to claim this new land ahead of the French or the Dutch, they paid little attention to the indigenous people who had been living there for at least twenty thousand years.

Arthur Phillip, governor of the penal colony, came up with the name *ab origine*—Latin for "original," or "first"—ironically ignoring the implication that the natives had prior claim to the land. Instead, the British government preferred to ignore the existence of the entire native population.

Many of the convicts had been transported from England for the crime of poaching (shooting or snaring game on land not their own). But when they arrived in Sydney Cove, no one thought twice about hunting and fishing on territory that was already inhabited. The "savages" were considered to be "mischievous" when they demanded, or simply took, what they assumed was their due from the game or fish the English had shot or netted.

The aboriginals' weapons were sticks and stones, or spears held together with tree gum. The only thing they killed was their dinners—kangaroos, emus, and fish. Until the arrival of the British, not one of them owned—or had ever seen—a gun. It was the guns that allowed the newcomers to tame these "savages" and to push them out of the way, slowly taking over the valuable coastal regions and lush farmland for themselves.

As time went by, white farmers and ranchers had more to worry about than displacing the aboriginals. Those five rabbits, originally brought over from England in 1787 with the First Fleet, had adapted happily to the climate and vegetation in the southern hemisphere. They had flourished, and reproduced so rapidly that by the early 1900's there were millions of them plaguing the continent, causing serious damage to crops. Their attempted solution was to build barriers to protect Western Australia from the intruding vermin.

For the indigenous people living in the Australian bush in 1901, the construction of a "rabbit-proof" fence cutting across the country north to south, from sea to sea, must have caused confusion and alarm. Their territory had already shrunk because of the white man's cities and farms. Now it was being cut up into fenced pieces as well. Even well-meaning white landowners apparently saw no irony when they offered "camps" as safe havens for the nomadic tribes who were threatened by the white man's encroaching civilization. But the camps made the Mardu and other kinship groups more vulnerable to another threat: their families could be found and dispersed more easily.

By the time the rabbit-proof fences, the longest in the world, were finally completed in 1907, the rabbits had easily crossed the boundary and were prolific on both sides. Government policy failed to restrain rabbits, but was far more successful in controlling the lives of human children. While the fence was being built against pesky rabbits, the Aborigines Act of 1905 was passed in Western Australia. This law, in an effort to place controls on the aboriginal population, determined that any child having one white parent and one dark-skinned aboriginal parent—a "half-caste"—could be forcibly removed from his or her family and placed in a Native Settlement to be educated. The government's hope was to prevent the expansion of a third race. The white men who enforced this policy were content to let full-blood aboriginal children remain in the care of their parents, but those with "mixed blood" were to be contained in state-run institutions, in the hope that they would eventually forget their heritage and native language and grow up as whole-hearted products of a white education. It was further intended that with careful monitoring of marriages and birthing, it would be possible to "breed out the colour" (a popular political term at the time) of the descendents of the half-caste population. The children taken from their families during this time became known as "the Stolen Generations." These were the dreadful years when both Molly and her daughter Doris were born.

The Rabbit-Proof Fence tells us that Molly's life began peacefully, in the midst of a large extended family. Her father, Thomas Craig, was a white man who worked as an inspector on the famous fence. Thomas had moved away, but Molly's mother, Maude (affectionately called Bambaru in Doris's memoir), had many siblings and cousins to help raise her children. "Daisy and Gracie were called *muda-muda* because, like Molly, their skin was not as dark as the other Mardu children. Their mothers were Molly's aunts. Their fathers were [also] white stockmen." Doris explains that being *muda-muda* often meant feeling like an outsider, even in their own camp.

Along with family memories, Doris introduces the reader to a feast of details about the traditions of the bush people, the beautiful landscape of Western Australia, how food was gathered and prepared, observations of animals and insects, and a familiarity with the flowers, bushes, and trees that signal the passage of the seasons. Sprinkled throughout her books, Doris uses many words of Mardu wangka, the language of her people, and helpfully provides a glossary, so the reader is certain to understand.

> Molly and her cousin Gracie . . . could join the women in the search for bush fruit and vegetables and digging for goannas, honey ants and *longkis,* known also as bardies, a tasty grub found in the roots of the Acacia trees. They used the digging stick as their main tool. If it was needed for protection, the same stick, or *wana,* was used as a weapon. Boys used boomerangs and spears when hunting emus, kangaroos, and wild turkeys. Nobody had guns.

But the white men (or *wudgebulla* in the Mardu language) had guns, and used them to control the aboriginals—to round them up, to decide where they should live, who they should marry, and to reclaim whichever children they thought would take Australia one step closer to being an all-white country.

Molly was a *durn-durn,* a girl who had reached puberty. She would already have been married, except that the man she'd been promised to had selected a different bride instead. She was fourteen on the terrible day when her life changed forever.

Mr. A. O. Neville, was the official Chief Protector of Aborigines, and, through the Act of 1905, legal guardian of all aboriginal children. Under his orders, an officer named Constable Riggs arrived at Molly's family camp near Jigalong. He had come to take "three half-caste girls" to the Moore River Native Settlement. Molly, with her cousin Gracie and sister Daisy, was swiftly removed from the only community she'd ever known.

"A high pitched wail broke out" as they departed. "The cries of ago-nized mothers . . . and the deep sobs of grandfathers, uncles and cousins filled the air. . . . Behind them, those remaining in the camp found strong sharp objects and gashed themselves and inflicted wounds to their heads and bodies as an expression of sorrow. This reaction to their children's abduction showed that the family were now in mourning."

Mr. Neville seems to have truly believed that once the Mardu of mixed blood understood the white man's intentions, they would be grateful for the opportunity to relinquish the nomadic life they'd grown up with. He later wrote: "The native must be helped in spite of himself! Even if a measure of discipline is necessary, it must be applied, but it can be applied in such a way as to appear to be gentle persuasion . . . the end in view will justify the means employed." Mr. Neville's definition of "gentle persuasion" certainly did not coincide with that of Molly's family.

Included in Doris's book are copies of several documents and tele-grams written by various officials. One letter, from a local Superintendent at the Government Depot at Jigalong, was sadly ignored: "These chil-dren lean more towards the black than white, and on second thought, [I] think nothing would be gained in removing them." This sentiment was echoed in a letter by an inspector in South Australia: "The natives have as much love and affection for their children as the white people have," he wrote, adding that the government's actions were "nothing short of kidnapping."

Once the initial shock of separation had subsided, the girls' jour-ney was actually full of novelty and astonishment. They traveled for sev-eral days: by train, on a boat, through the huge city of Perth—all things they'd never done before. The trip took nearly a week, but arrival at their new home was even more dismaying than they'd expected. The children slept in dormitories, were given strange food, and were forced to wear shoes and cover themselves up with uncomfortable clothing, which felt very unnatural. The so-called caregivers did not seem to care at all.

Within a few days of arriving, Molly saw that the weather was ideal for escape. It was chilly and drizzling, meaning that the rain would soon wash their tracks away. Molly told the others to save the bread crusts usually scorned at breakfast. "They snatched up their meager possessions and put them into calico bags and pulled the long drawstrings and slung them around their necks. Each one put on two dresses, two pairs of calico bloomers and a coat. Then they left the coats behind, too heavy to carry."

Their first obstacle was the rain-swollen river that bordered the settlement's property. But Molly kept to the banks until they found a fallen tree that acted as a bridge. The other girls "followed her muddy footprints in silence without any questions, trusting her leadership totally."

Once they were across, Molly said, "We go *kyalie* [north] now all the way." She figured out that if they could find the rabbit-proof fence, it would lead them home to Jigalong.

On their first night out, they came across an empty rabbit burrow and Molly decided it would make a good camp.

Crouching on their knees, they dug furiously with their elbows almost touching each other's. Very soon they managed to widen and deepen a deserted burrow to make a slightly cramped but warm dry shelter. . . . Crawling in one at a time, they cuddled up together in the rabbit burrow, wriggling and twisting around until they were comfortable. . . . The next morning very early, the three girls were awakened by the thump, thumping of rabbits from adjoining burrows.

Gracie was quick to catch and kill one, but because they had no matches to light a fire, they reluctantly abandoned the dead rabbit and kept walking.

During the next several weeks, these three brave girls passed through territories they'd never seen before: wet grasslands, more rivers, open landscape, giant marri gum trees with thick trunks, prickly dense undergrowth, white sand, tidy farms, and heath lands carpeted with blooming flowers.

They had encounters with many strangers, some who helped and some who hindered their flight. Early on, they met a pair of Mardu men returning from a hunting trip who gave them a roasted kangaroo tail to share, and the greater treasures of matches and salt, along with a warning that the officials from Moore River were still searching for the girls. "'They got a Mardu policeman, a proper cheeky fullah. He flog 'em young runaway gels like you three.'" This was a good reminder to Molly that she'd need to be cunning to outsmart an aboriginal tracker. The gift of matches meant that the next time they caught rabbits, "they made a huge fire in a hole in the ground and cooked the rabbits in the ashes, after gutting them roughly by using a sharp point of a green stick."

The girls faced plenty of reasons for their spirits to slip—rain, rain, and more rain, scary giant kangaroos, search planes passing overhead, tired feet, and infected sores on their legs.

Weary and weak with hunger, they one day warily approached a farmhouse and were rewarded with what seemed like a feast from a woman named Mrs. Flanagan. She also told them the dismal news that they were walking in the wrong direction! She supplied them with mutton and tomato chutney sandwiches on crusty bread, fruitcake, and sweet, milky tea. She filled brown paper bags with tea leaves, sugar, flour, and salt, along with more mutton, bread, cake, billycans, and coats. She dug out some old wheat bags to use as rain capes.

After the girls had continued on their way, Mrs. Flanagan must have worried that they wouldn't survive. She broke her promise to Molly and reported the visit to the authorities. Molly, however, had already guessed that no one should be trusted, least of all a *midgerji*—a white woman. She led Daisy and Gracie in the same wrong direction for a couple of hours before doubling back to continue the right way. They used this trick whenever they neared a farmhouse—approach from one direction and leave in another, always sneaking around later to follow the right path.

At last they spied the rabbit-proof fence. Not knowing that after eight hundred kilometers they were still only halfway home, Molly "greeted the fence like a long-lost friend, touching and gripping the cold wire. . . . It would stand out like a beacon that would lead them out of the rugged wilderness across a strange country to their homeland."

When the younger girls began to suffer intolerable leg pain, Molly carried them in turns. They encountered an aboriginal man riding a bicycle, who informed the searchers where he'd spotted them. But luck was again on their side; heavy rains erased their footprints so that the tracker couldn't follow. They stopped lighting fires and took more care, knowing that even as they crept closer to home, they were still in great danger of being caught.

Gracie, the eleven-year-old, finally faltered. When a farmwife told her that her mother had come searching to a nearby town, Gracie insisted that she detour to find her mother instead of continuing to Jigalong. Molly argued fiercely to convince her of how dangerous this might be, but Gracie insisted. The girls said good-bye to each other near the train station in Wiluna. Molly and Daisy would not know until later that Gracie was captured within a day and returned to Moore River. They now pressed onward, more determined than ever to make their way home.

Molly and Daisy arrived at the house of Molly's stepfather's sister. They were welcomed with open arms, a real bath, and hot beef stew, though their stomachs had shrunk during their ordeal and they were not able to eat very much. After a day's rest, they began the final part of the journey. They didn't have to walk the last few miles home; their uncle let them ride his camel.

Nine weeks and 1,600 kilometers had passed since they had been torn away from their family. They were welcomed like long-lost heroes, but slept there only one night. Early the next morning, the whole group moved to a distant camp in the desert—no one wanted to risk the recapture of the two brave girls.

Molly managed to roam with her family and remain hidden from the authorities until she was safely beyond sixteen, the age when children were no longer eligible for the re-settlement program. She had a white sweetheart, and then a half-caste boyfriend, before an arranged marriage with an aboriginal husband named Toby. Toby and Molly worked for Bill and Mary Dunnet at the Balfour Downs station, a ranch where sheep and cattle were raised.

Baby Doris was born early and came as a surprise. No other women were around so Molly's eight-year-old cousin helped to deliver the baby. Molly found a place under a wintamarra tree, laid down a blanket, and gave birth. She cut her own umbilical cord using a butcher's knife.

Molly named her daughter Nugi Garimara. But her employer, Mary Dunnet, told her, "That's a stupid name. Give her a proper name. Call her Doris."

The new baby weighed just three pounds and looked "like a tiny skinned rabbit." Her first bed was a shoebox and her first milk was given through an eyedropper. No one, including the doctor, expected her to live more than a few days, but she gained weight and grew into a strong little girl. She was particularly attached to her grandmother, Bambaru, who had become blind several years earlier from an affliction related to the sand that blew in the desert. Despite her very young age, Doris became her grandmother's seeing eyes, watching the fire, gathering bush foods, and even helping to roast freshly killed kangaroos.

When Doris was three and a half, with an eight-month-old baby sister named Anna, her mother had an attack of appendicitis. Molly could not go to the local hospital because it did not treat aboriginal people. The Commissioner of Native Affairs saw an opportunity to "recover" two more children and gave approval for Molly to get treatment at the hospital in the town of Perth, as long as the "black husband" got left behind. To avoid Molly's objections or even disappearance, she wasn't told about the plan until the mail truck showed up to transport her to the train. In a traumatic repetition of history, she was dragged away from her home and circle of relatives, this time with her daughters, too.

"Having his wife and two daughters taken from him was too much for Toby to bear. Beside him, wailing louder than the rest, was Bambaru, whose bright red blood poured from a self-inflicted wound on her head, which was her people's traditional way of expressing deep mourning for the loss of loved ones." Bambaru, broken-hearted and missing her beloved granddaughter—and eyes—died a year later without ever meeting her again.

Once Molly had recovered from the removal of her appendix, she learned the distressing truth—that she would not be permitted to take her daughters home. They were now the "property" of the government. Molly immediately applied for a job as a cook at Moore River so that she could be near her precious girls while she considered what to do. "Women were permitted to talk to their children but physical contact was not allowed."

Each day Doris would wait for her mother's visit in a particular place beside the high steel interlock fence that separated the kindergarten children from the others. "She knew what time to sit down and wait, she was told to watch for a certain time of the day when the sun reached a special place in the sky."

One day, Molly and Anna did not appear. It was over a year since they had arrived at Moore River. All that time the authorities had kept careful watch over Molly, knowing she had escaped once before. Finally they had relaxed their guard, giving Molly the chance she'd been patiently waiting for. Ten years after her original notorious escape, Molly sneaked away again, carrying baby Anna. She had no choice but to leave Doris, trapped behind that high wire fence.

This time, Molly was luckier than during her childhood escapade: halfway home, she met a sympathetic fence worker who gave her a lift in his jeep the rest of the way. But of course her troubles were not over.

The Commissioner of Native Affairs was irate about Molly being a runaway, mostly because he wanted to hang on to her child. He wrote to the Balfour Downs Station that although Molly would be allowed to live with her husband again, "the little girl Anna is too white to remain in the native environment. She will have to be brought back to Moore River."

Molly managed to stay out of reach for two more years, but then she and Anna were admitted to hospital, both with eye infections. Anna's infection was severe and she was detained a long while, during which time Molly worked at the hospital, intending to stay close by. Finally, though, Anna was taken away by officials and installed at the Sister Kates Children's Home in Perth. Molly never saw her again.

And what happened to Doris during all this time?

Fortunately, when Doris got left behind at the Moore River settlement, her Aunty Gracie was one of the caregivers assigned to look after her. This helped a bit with the panic and sorrow of separation. She had a few friends by day, but the nights were miserable—in a cot with bars instead of snuggled with Bambaru or Mummy. The explanation given by some of the people in charge was "Your mother doesn't love you."

The dreadful food served up in the institution was just the same as in Molly's day: porridge full of weevils (a kind of small bug), and watery stews. Doris and her best friends, Tony and Andrew Onslow, had grown up in the bush, accustomed to helping their elders forage for food. Now, they occasionally did some gathering of their own. Doris records incidents of eating dried out carrots or banana skins—things that would have been entirely acceptable "bush food" among their families. But she and the boys were jeered at and called "rubbish eaters." Doris couldn't understand how "rubbish" food was any worse than what was offered on the settlement tables!

Part of the effort to assimilate the children into the white community was to forbid them to use their native languages. Doris, as Molly had before her, struggled with this. "'You're a very naughty girl, you must not talk blackfella language again,' yelled Nurse Hannah," to Doris.

Slowly, Doris began to lose her connection with her own past. She recalls one day when she saw a blazing bonfire on the grounds of the settlement. She raced toward it, vivid memories stirred up of Bambaru and her childhood. Her moment of joy led to severe punishment, part of the vigorous routine to erase cultural ties for aboriginal children. After the fire incident, Doris consciously decided to suppress her memories because they only led to getting smacked.

Meanwhile, the government made another decision that would affect her future. The Moore River Settlement School was closed, and Doris was sent, with thirty-one other girls, to the Roelands Native Mission.

"Then one beautiful spring afternoon, Matron handed Doris a letter; and because the mail was opened and censored, she had no idea where it came from. Doris fought back the tears as she read the letter; her first letter from her own mother."

They began to correspond, but were not yet able to meet. Doris finished school and trained as a nurse. Finally, after she was a wife with four small children of her own, Doris traveled back to Jigalong. The train ride was a long one, followed by a tiring walk. She stopped to ask directions and was told, "'Your mother is camping at that last house. . . . You'll know her; she's the only half-caste woman there.'"

Doris spoke her first words to her mother after twenty-three years: "'Do you know me?'" Then she asked, "'Why did you give me away, Mum?'" Her mother was quick to answer: "'I didn't give you away! You were taken . . .'" Doris had not realized until that minute that their separation had been against her mother's will.

Meeting her father was just as emotional.

"'This is your Daddy,' said her mother tenderly." Holding her baby daughter, Doris embraced her father. "His hand brushed the hair from Doris's cheek. His fingers traced her brow, stopping at the indentation, the identifying mark, made so many years ago in the attack by the cattle dog at Balfour Downs. His child, Nugi, had come home."

⌢

Centuries earlier, Margaret Catchpole had come to the place that Doris's people called home, a reluctant trespasser from her native land. But even in her own country, Doris, too, was made to feel like a stranger, forced to live inside another culture. Both these women, along with the others in this book, used words to map unfamiliar territory until their stories— fictional or factual—became part of history.

To End

I have lived with the women in this book for three years while writing their stories. Brave, clever, and spirited, I feel I know them well by now, and have grown to love them. I shake my head in wonder at their remarkable lives.

But, these are only *eleven* remarkable lives. Each one has made me curious to keep reading.

Following Sei's example, I have made a list of my own.

Things I want to know more about:
- Japanese footwear
- The first dentist in Australia
- The whereabouts of the slave girl brought home from Copang
- Painted portraits of African Americans
- The popularity of swans on supper menus
- Cannibals
- Monkeys as pets
- Life as a governess
- How Wrangel Island will be affected by climate change
- Snakes in Vietnam
- Aboriginal people still living in the Australian bush

What would you put on your list? What are you curious about? What will your own story be? Get scribbling . . .

NOTES

Sᴇɪ Sʜᴏɴᴀɢᴏɴ

Abbreviations:
PBIM: Sei Shonagon, *The Pillow Book of Sei Shonagon*. Edited and translated by Ivan Morris (New York: Columbia University Press, 1991).
PBMM: Sei Shonagon, *The Pillow Book*. Translated by Meredith McKinney (London: Penguin Books, 2006).

I really can't	PBMM, p. 208
Where else would	PBIM, p. 231
The years have passed	PBIM, p. 36
Ugly handwriting	PBIM, p. 71
Things that cannot	PBIM, p. 81
The man you love	PBMM, p. 59
things that just keep	PBMM, p. 205
Repulsive things	PBMM, p.151
Occasions for anxious	PBMM, p. 154
Elegant things	PBIM, p. 69
Pleasing things	PBIM, p. 218
Hateful things	PBIM, p. 44-46
I particularly despise	PBMM, p. 205
If letters did not	PBIM, p. 207
Sei Shonagon has	Murasaki Shikibu, *Diary of Lady Murasaki*. Cited at: http://www.newworldencyclopedia.org/entry/ Sei_Shonagon.
if I happen	PBMM, p. 212

Margaret Catchpole

Abbreviations:

NSW: Letters in collection of the Library of New South Wales

IpM: Letters in collection of the Ipswich Museum (Copyright Colchester and Ipswich Museum Service)

ipswich may 25	IpM
which she rode from	Bury and Norwich Post Newspaper Archives, August 16, 1797
dressed in a	Bury and Norwich Post Newspaper Archives, April 2, 1800
she again received	Bury and Norwich Post Newspaper Archives, August 6, 1800
at least one could	Robert Hughes, *The Fatal Shore* (New York: Alfred A. Knopf, 1987), p. 77.
honred madam	NSW
it is a Grat	NSW
FOR I MUST SAY	NSW
general muster	NSW
they have their	NSW
Norfolk Island	NSW
Madam be so kind	NSW
Barker is alive	NSW
To Dr. Stebbins	NSW
the Blacks, the natives	NSW
I hope, my good lady	NSW
By this day	NSW
fifteen shillings	NSW
hoping they are	NSW
hoping that I should	NSW
comfort it would be	NSW
This is a very	NSW
I am in great	NSW

He was for life	NSW
just very white	NSW
so I must conclude	NSW
I keep myself free	NSW
shoes 10 and 13	NSW
If you have any	NSW
I am almost	NSW
Honored Madam	NSW
I hav Lorst all my frunt	NSW
i am Liven	NSW
I was tossed	NSW

MARY HAYDEN RUSSELL

All quotes are from Letter-Journals of Mary (Hayden) Russell and Captain Forman Marshall Mount, 1823–1824 (unpublished), in the collection of the Nantucket Historical Association.

HARRIET JACOBS

Abbreviations:

HJAL: Jean Fagan Yellin, *Harriet Jacobs: A Life* (New York: Basic Civitas Books, 2004).

ILSG: Harriet Jacobs, *Incidents in the Life of a Slave Girl* (New York: New American Library, 2000).

I was born	ILSG. p. 1
Whereas the teaching . . . not exceeding thirty-nine	*A Bill to Prevent All Persons from Teaching Slaves to Read or Write, the Use of Figures Excepted* (1830-31 session of the General Assembly of the State of North Carolina).
fondly shielded	ILSG, p.1

I could not help	ILSG, p. 4
after a brief period	ILSG, p. 4
I would give much	ILSG, p. 8
While I was with	ILSG, p. 5
She awakened to	ILSG, p.17
They thought he	ILSG, p. 7
My master began	ILSG, p. 27
He told me	ILSG, p. 27
I loved him	ILSG, p. 38
I will shoot him	ILSG, p. 41
I will have you	ILSG, p. 38
The secrets of	ILSG, p. 35
nothing annoyed them	ILSG, p. 69
I arranged every thing	ILSG, p.69
He rushed from	ILSG, p.85
When they told me	ILSG, p. 85
I had many sad	ILSG, p. 95
to be broke in	ILSG, p. 95
At half past	ILSG, p. 106
I feared the sight	ILSG, p. 107
my pursuers came	ILSG, p. 109
the search for me	ILSG, p. 108
I received a message	ILSG, p. 111
Wherever you are	ILSG, p. 113
The darkest cloud	ILSG, p. 123
Put your hands	ILSG, p. 125
I was to remain	ILSG, p. 126
I saw snake	ILSG, p. 126-127
You must make	ILSG, p. 127
O, those long	ILSG, p.131
limbs were benumbed	ILSG, p. 136
trustworthy seafaring	ILSG, p. 142
She no longer felt	HJA, p. 57
with such feelings	ILSG, p. 158

I never could tell	ILSG, p. 176
O, the beautiful	ILSG, p. 179
I found the shops	ILSG, p. 181
One day she took	ILSG, p. 184
I was, in fact	ILSG, p. 218
I cannot say	ILSG, p. 220
I am rejoiced	ILSG, p. 225
My brain reeled	ILSG, p. 225
If God has bestowed	ILSG, p. 28
Why are ye silent	ILSG, p. 30
I can testify	ILSG, p. 56

ISABELLA BEETON

Abbreviations:

BoHM: Mrs. Isabella Beeton, *Mrs. Beeton's Book of Household Management*, abridged edition. Edited by Nicola Humble (Oxford: Oxford University Press, 2000).

EDM: *The Englishwoman's Domestic Magazine*. London: S.O. Beeton, 1852-1879.

a brush made	BoHM item #2313
there was an immense	"Isabella and Sam," in J. Limbird, publisher, *Mirror of Literature, Amusement, and Instruction* (London: 1822–1850), p. 36.
that living cargo	letter from Bella to Sam, cited in "Isabella and Sam," *Mirror of Literature, Amusement, and Instruction*, p. 38.
we shall get on	Letter from Bella to Sam (May 26, 1856), cited in Kathryn Hughes, *The Short Life and Long Times of Mrs. Beeton, the First Domestic Goddess* (New York: Alfred A. Knopf, 2006), p. 119.
Yours most. . . . Yours with all	Letters from Bella to Sam (spring 1856), cited in *The Short life & Long Times of Mrs.Beeton*, p. 99.

To Wives and Housekeepers	EDM, 1857
it is upon her	BoHM, item #79
Cut round the top	Cited on: http://www.ideafinder.com/history/inventions/canopener.htm
I must frankly own	BoHM, "Preface"
Dine we must	BoHM, item #1882
What moved me	BoHM, "Preface"
As with the commander	BoHM, item #1
The bread in the	BoHM, item #1776
a plain statement	BoHM, "Preface"
Honey Cake	BoHM, item #1758
Baked flour, when cooked	BoHM, item #2500
let them eat meat	BoHM, item #2415
Toast Sandwiches	BoHM, item #1877
for boiling, choose	BoHM, item # 977
A great authority	BoHM, item #1761
descriptions: square face, sleek Doctor, etc.	Isabella's diary, cited in *Short Life and Long Times*, p. 256.
A place for	BoHM, item #55
Box of Chocolate	BoHM, item #1602

MARY KINGSLEY

Abbreviations:

TiWA: Mary Kingsley, *Travels in West Africa* (Mineola, New York: Dover, 2003).

You are coming	TiWA, p. 38
Most Notorious	Katherine Frank, *A Voyager Out: The Life of Mary Kingsley* (New York: Ballantine Books, 1986), p. 15.
she wore mourning	BBC 4 radio interview, *Great Lives,* with Dea Burkett, biographer.

she wrote every	BBC 4 radio interview, *Great Lives,* with Dea Burkett, biographer.
I have always been	Letter to Matthew Nathan, cited in *A Voyager Out,* p. 269.
long, waterproof	TiWA, p. 4
The opening sentence	TiWA, p. 5
Deadliest spot	TiWA p. 2
The dangers of	TiWA p. 2
I went down	Letter to Matthew Nathan, cited in *A Voyager Out,* p. xix.
I fully expected	TiWA, p. 5
Whenever and however	TiWA, p. 13
in a way more	TiWA, p. 16
and half a hundred	TiWA, p. 22
animal descriptions	TiWA, p. 23-24
African culture	TiWA, p. 220
Next in danger	TiWA, p. 689
Oh! We always keep	TiWA, p. 32
This dish is really	TiWA, p. 228
The first day	TiWA, p. 265
A crocodile drifting	TiWA, p. 88
I saw . . . wading	TiWA, p. 258
horrible disgust	TiWA, p. 268, footnote
I have seen many	TiWA, p. 268
The leopard crouched.	TiWA, p. 545
for remember that	TiWA, p. 196
Hippo flesh is not	TiWA, p. 196
our souls, unliberated	TiWA, p. 189
We were two hours	TiWA, p. 303
My face and particularly	TiWA, p. 582
I just take a	TiWA, p. 601
Conversation and	TiWA, p. 127
I retired into	TiWA, p. 128
The next news was	TiWA, p. 269

I shook hands with   TiWA, p.271

I then shook its   TiWA, p. 273

although the Fans   TiWA, p. 273

The cannibalism   TiWA, p. 330

The rain now began   TiWA, p. 579

we limp in   TiWA, p. 597

I write by the light   TiWA, p. 572

I believe if   TiWA, p. 586

a burst of bitter   TiWA, p. 594

Don't fall, I yelled   TiWA, p. 607

Head man and I   TiWA, p. 598

a black man is no   TiWA, p. 659

She complained   Rebecca Stefoff, *Women of the World: Women Travelers and Explorers* (New York: Oxford University Press, 1992), p. 80.

as brief as possible   Adam Hochschild, *King Leopold's Ghost: A Story of Greed, Terror, and Heroism in Colonial Africa* (Boston: Houghton Mifflin, 1998), p. 71.

the African at large   TiWA, p. 673

You hear, nearer to   Lecture, cited in *A Voyager Out*, p. 90.

the coffin, wrongly   http://www.billgreenwell.com

One by one I took   TiWA, p. 6

NELLIE BLY

Abbreviations:

72D: Nellie Bly, *Around the World in 72 Days* (New York: The Pictorial Weeklies Company, 1890). http://digital.library.upenn.edu/women/bly/world/world.html.

10D: Nellie Bly, *Ten Days in a Mad House* (New York: Ian L. Munro, Publisher, no date). (Online version: http://digital.library.upenn.edu/women/bly/madhouse/madhouse.html)

My teeth chattered   10D, Ch. XI

restless, dissatisfied   Erasmus Wilson, "Quiet Observer," *Pittsburg Dispatch*. Cited in Brooke Kroeger, *Nellie Bly: Daredevil, Reporter, Feminist* (New York: Times Books, Random House, 1994), p. 41.

home a little   Erasmus Wilson, "Quiet Observer," *Pittsburg Dispatch*. Cited in Brooke Kroeger.

there is no greater   Erasmus Wilson, "Quiet Observer," *Pittsburg Dispatch*. Cited in Brooke Kroeger.

without talent   "Nellie Bly, The Girl Puzzle," *Pittsburg Dispatch*, January 25, 1885. Cited in Brooke Kroeger, p. 41.

paid father's doctor   "Nellie Bly, The Girl Puzzle," *Pittsburg Dispatch*, cited in Kroeger, p. 41.

Just as smart   "Nellie Bly, The Girl Puzzle," *Pittsburg Dispatch*, cited in Kroeger, p. 42.

women have a problem   *American Experience: Around the World in 72 Days*, Written, produced, and directed by Christine Lesiak. PBS, 2005.

I said I could   10D, Ch. I

tenderly I put   10D, Ch. II

From a directory   10D, Ch. II

a small tin plate   10D, Ch. VI

in spite of the knowledge . . .   10D, Ch. VIII

But here let me   10D, Ch. I

I was hungry   10D, Ch. XI

In our short walks   10D, Ch. XII

I came in and saw   10D, Ch. XI

For crying the nurses   10D, Ch. XIV

I went to the bathtub   10D, Ch. XI

Can you imagine   10D, Ch. XII

to take a perfectly   10D, Ch. XII

It was my custom   72D, Ch. I

"Very well," I said   72D, Ch. I

I always have a	72D, Ch. I
I was able to pack	72D, Ch. I
I had such a strong	72D, Ch. I
Then to encourage	72D, Ch. II
I think it is only natural	72D, Ch. II
Jules Verne's bright	72D, Ch. III
which gave me	72D, Ch. IV
my line of travel	72D, Ch. IV
If you do it	72D, Ch. IV
Occasionally we	72D, Ch. VI
Before the boat	72D, Ch. VII
hardly had the	72D, Ch. VII
what looked like	72D, Ch. VII
black fellows . . . have	72D, Ch. VIII
tree branches	72D, Ch. VIII
the tooth-destroying	72D, Ch. VIII
half a dozen	From "Jersey Back to Jersey," *The New York World*, January 26, 1890.
You are going to be	72D, Ch. XII
the best reporter	*The New York World*, January 25, 1922.

DAISY ASHFORD

Abbreviations:

YV: Daisy Ashford, *The Young Visiters or Mr. Salteena's Plan* (Garden City: Doubleday & Company, Inc, 1919).

DA Her Book: Daisy Ashford, *Daisy Ashford. Her Book*. With a preface by Irvin S. Cobb (New York: George H. Doran Company, 1920).

LDA: R. M. Malcomson, *Daisy Ashford; Her Life* (London: Chatto & Windus—The Hogarth Press, 1984).

I adored writing	Daisy Ashford, cited by J. M. Barrie in preface to YV.
I like a rainy	Daisy Ashford, cited in LDA, p. 76.

Dear Auntie	Daisy Ashford, cited in LDA, p. 49.
So with hands	LDA, p. 52
The butler informs	LDA, p. 81
Mr. Salteena was	YV, p. 17
Mr. Salteena had	YV, p. 17
Ethel Monticue had	YV, p. 17
quear shaped	YV, p. 17
My Dear Alfred	YV, p. 18
I am not quite	YV, p. 19
A tall man of 29	YV, p. 26
Oh yes gasped	YV, p. 26
nervously wishing	YV, p. 54
rich satin with	YV, p. 83
of pure lace	YV, p. 83
jam tarts with	YV, p. 85
everybody got a	YV, p. 88
I put so much	Daisy Ashford, foreword to DA Her Book.
Bernard Clark	was YV, p. 92

ADA BLACKJACK

Abbreviations:

DDART: The Papers of Ada Blackjack, in the Dartmouth College Library.

SDART: Ada Blackjack statement to E. R. Jorgenson (made in Seattle, February 6, 1924) in collection at Dartmouth College Library.

AB/JN: Jennifer Niven, *Ada Blackjack; A True Story of Survival in the Arctic* (New York: Hyperion, 2003).

One day just after	SDART
she was barely	Jennifer Niven, in a statement for *National Geographic News,* January 15, 2004.
the fellows started	from the diary of Lorne Knight, cited in Vilhjalmur Stefansson, *The Adventure of Wrangel*

	Island (New York: The MacMillan Company, 1925).
I think that anyone	Stefansson, cited in AB/JN, p.19.
The report was grim	Cited in AB/JN, p. 119.
The boys expected	SDART
This means merely	Letter from Stefansson to Harry Galle, cited in AB/JN p. 121.
At Christmas time	SDART
made a calendar	SDART
she's bunk	Lorne Knight diary (March 3, 1923), cited in AB/JN, p. 166.
Made in March	DDART
March 16th	DDART
26th . . . I haul	DDART
It has caught	DDART
If anything happen	DDART
and when I come	DDART
And he menitions	DDART
If I be known dead	DDART
Apr. 22 I didn't	DDART
Apr. 29th still blowing	DDART
I was out to chop	DDART
He was so weak	SDART
He had a one-pound	SDART
I think he was	DDART
I fry one biscuit	DDART
blanked coat	DDART
clothe parky	DDART
see gall	DDART
I know she love	DDART
I just write	DDART
knight is very	DDART
I found one	DDART
June 17th I wash	DDART

June 21 . . . knight	DDART
Dear Galle	*The Literary Digest,* December 8, 1923, cited in AB/JN, p. 208.
June 22. I move	DDART
Wrangel Island	Ada's typewritten pages, DART, cited in AB/JN, p. 209.
I had hard time	SDART
I took pictures	DDART
I saw a seal	DDART
saw Polar bear	DDART
July 1st	I stay DDART
all day very nice	DDART
it works all right	DDART
July 19	. . . the beach DDART
oh yes I dreamed	DDART
I clean seal flappers	DDART
July 30 . . . the ice	DDART
I made another	DDART
Aug. 20	DDART
Real history is	Letter from Mae Belle Anderson to Helen Crawford, cited in AB/JN, p. 2.

Dang Thuy Tram

Abbreviations:
PEACE: Dang Thuy Tram, *Last Night I Dreamed of Peace; The Diary of Dang Thuy Tram.* Translated by Andrew X. Pham (New York: Harmony Books, 2007).
HIEN: Statement by Hien Tram, from a personal memoir.

5th November	PEACE, p. 162
fun stuff from	HIEN
singing and	HIEN
usually had to	HIEN

April 8, 1968	Operated PEACE, p. 4
22 April, 1968. Huong died?	PEACE, p. 11
July comes again	PEACE, p. 30
The cold wind	PEACE, p. 51
17th May 1968 The war	PEACE, p. 20
4th June 1968 Rain falls	PEACE, p. 26
I alone am	PEACE, p. 37
28 July . . . Brother	PEACE, p. 39
4th August . . . Sister	PEACE, p. 41
27 September	1968 . . . I've been PEACE, p. 55
25 August 1969 . . . Sister Thu Huong	PEACE, p. 149
26 November . . . Another year	PEACE, p.165
20th June . . . Today there is only	PEACE, p.224
Don't burn this	Telephone interview with Fred Whitehurst, March 12, 2010.
a collection of	PEACE, Foreword by Frances Fitzgerald, p. xvi
what I was doing	Telephone interview with Fred Whitehurst, March 12, 2010.
I felt as if	Dang Ngoc Tram, cited at: http://www.npr.org/templates/story/story.php?storyId=6492819.

DORIS PILKINGTON GARIMARA

Abbreviations:

RPF: Doris Pilkington Garimara, *Rabbit-Proof Fence* (New York: Hyperion Miramax Books, 2002).

UWT: Doris Pilkington Garimara, *Under the Wintamarra Tree* (Queensland: University of Queensland Press, 2002).

One day in a   RPF, p. 113

I began writing   E-mail interview with Doris Pilkington Garimara,
                        summer 2009.

Daisy and Gracie   Doris Pilkington Garimara, *Home to Mother*
                        (Queensland: University of Queensland Press,
                        2006). p. 3.

Molly and her   *Home to Mother*, p. 2

three half-caste   RPF, p. 44

A high pitched wail   RPF, p. 44

This reaction to their RPF, p. 45

The native must be helped Auber Octavius Neville, *Australia's Coloured
                        Minority: Its Place in the Community* (Sydney:
                        Currawong Publishing Company, 1947), p. 80.

These children   Mr. A.J. Keeling, superintendant's report, cited in
                        RPF, p. 61.

The natives have as much Inspector Thomas Clode, letter, 14 February,
                        1910. Cited as part of Human Rights and Equal
                        Opportunity Commission (Australia), *Bringing
                        Them Home—Report of the National Inquiry into the
                        Separation of Aboriginal and Torres Strait Islander
                        Children from Their Families*, April 1997.

They snatched up   RPF, p. 78

followed her muddy   RPF, p. 81

we go *kyalie*   RPF, p. 81

crouching on their knees RPF, p. 86

They got a Mardu   RPF, p. 91

They made a huge   RPF, p. 94

greeted the fence   RPF, p. 110

That's a stupid   UWT, p. 29

like a tiny skinned   UWT, p. 25

black husband   UWT, p. 55

having his wife   UWT, pp. 55-56

women were permitted   UWT, p. 77

She knew what   UWT, p.78

the little girl	UWT, p. 61
You're a very	UWT, p. 82
Then one beautiful	UWT, p. 144
Your mother is	UWT, p. 180
Do you know me?	UWT, p. 181
I didn't give	UWT, p. 185
This is your	UWT, p. 185

SELECTED BIBLIOGRAPHY

Books

Ashford, Daisy. *Daisy Ashford: Her Book*. With a preface by Irvin S. Cobb. New York: George H. Doran Company, 1920.

Ashford, Daisy. *The Young Visiters or Mr. Salteena's Plan*. Garden City: Doubleday & Company, Inc, 1919.

Beeton, Mrs. Isabella. *Mrs. Beeton's Book of Household Management*, abridged edition. Edited by Nicola Humble. Oxford: Oxford University Press, 2000.

Birkett, Dea. *Spinsters Abroad; Victorian Lady Explorers*. London: Victor Gollancz Ltd, 1991.

Bly, Nellie. *Around the World in 72 Days*. New York: The Pictorial Weeklies Company, 1890. http://digital.library.upenn.edu/women/bly/world/world.html

Bly, Nellie. *Ten Days in a Mad House*. New York: Ian L. Munro, Publisher, no date. (Online version: http://digital.library.upenn.edu/women/bly/madhouse/madhouse.html)

Bollmann, Stefan. *Women Who Write*. With an introduction by Francine Prose. London: Merrell, 2007.

Catchpole, Margaret. Letters in collection of the Ipswich Museum (Copyright Colchester and Ipswich Museum Service).

Catchpole, Margaret. Letters in collection of the Library of New South Wales.

Cobbold, Richard. *History of Margaret Catchpole; a Suffolk Girl.* London: Oxford University Press, 1845.

Cordingly, David. *Seafaring Women: Adventures of Pirate Queens, Female Stowaways, and Sailors' Wives.* New York: Random House, 2001.

Dang, Thuy Tram. *Last Night I Dreamed of Peace; The Diary of Dang Thuy Tram.* Translated by Andrew X Pham. New York: Harmony Books, 2007.

Ehrenreich, Barbara and Deirdre English. *Witches, Midwives and Nurses: A History of Women Healers.* New York: The Feminist Press, 1973.

Emerson, Kathy Lyn. *Making Headlines: A Biography of Nellie Bly.* Minneapolis: Dillon Press, 1989.

The Englishwoman's Domestic Magazine. London: S.O. Beeton, 1852-1879.

Frank, Katherine. *A Voyager Out: The Life of Mary Kingsley.* New York: Ballantine Books, 1986.

Garimara, Doris Pilkington. *Caprice, a Stockman's Daughter.* Queensland: University of Queensland Press, 2002.

Garimara, Doris Pilkington. *Home to Mother.* Queensland: University of Queensland Press, 2006.

Garimara, Doris Pilkington. *Rabbit-Proof Fence.* New York: Hyperion Miramax Books, 2002.

Garimara, Doris Pilkington. *Under the Wintamarra Tree.* Queensland: University of Queensland Press, 2002.

Grant, R.G. *The African-American Slave Trade*. New York: Barron's Educational Series, Inc. 2003.

Hochschild, Adam. *King Leopold's Ghost: A Story of Greed, Terror, and Heroism in Colonial Africa*. Boston: Houghton Mifflin, 1998.

Hughes, Kathryn. *The Short Life and Long Times of Mrs. Beeton, the First Domestic Goddess*. New York: Alfred A. Knopf, 2006.

Hughes, Robert. *The Fatal Shore*. New York: Alfred A. Knopf, 1987.

Hyde, H. Montgomery. *Mr. and Mrs. Beeton*. Edinborough: Harrap, 1951.

Jacobs, Harriet. *Incidents in the Life of a Slave Girl*. New York: New American Library, 2000.

Keneally, Thomas. *A Commonwealth of Thieves: The Improbable Birth of Australia*. New York: Nan A. Talese/Doubleday, 2006.

Kingsley, Mary. *Travels in West Africa*. Mineola, New York: Dover, 2003.

Kroeger, Brooke. *Nellie Bly: Daredevil, Reporter, Feminist*. New York: Times Books, Random House, 1994.

Limbird, J., publisher. *Mirror of Literature, Amusement, and Instruction* (London: 1822–1850).

Lyons, Mary E. *Keeping Secrets; The Girlhood Diaries of Seven Women Writers*. New York: Henry Holt and Company, Inc, 1995.

Lyons, Mary E. *Letters from a Slave Girl: The Story of Harriet Jacobs*. New York: Simon and Schuster, 1992.

Malcomson, R. M. *Daisy Ashford; Her Life*. London: Chatto & Windus—The Hogarth Press, 1984.

Manning-Sanders. *The Extraordinary Margaret Catchpole*. London: Heinemann, 1966.

Neville, Auber Octavius. *Australia's Coloured Minority: Its Place in the Community*. Sydney: Currawong Publishing Company, 1947.

Niven, Jennifer. *Ada Blackjack; A True Story of Survival in the Arctic*. New York: Hyperion, 2003.

Philbrick, Nathaniel. *In the Heart of the Sea*. New York: Penguin Books, 2000.

Philbrick, Nathaniel. *Revenge of the Whale; The True Story of the Whaleship* Essex. New York: G.P. Putnam's Sons, 2002.

Reader's Digest. *Everyday Life Through the Ages*. London: The Reader's Digest Association Limited, 1992.

Rees, Sian. *The Floating Brothel: The extraordinary true story of an 18th century ship and its cargo of female convicts*. London: Headline Book Publishing, 2001.

Shikibu, Murasaki. *Diary of Lady Murasaki*. Cited at:http://www.new-worldencyclopedia.org/entry/ Sei_Shonagon.

Shonagon, Sei. *The Pillow Book*. Translated by Meredith McKinney. London: Penguin Books, 2006.

Shonagon, Sei. *The Pillow Book of Sei Shonagon*. Edited and translated by Ivan Morris. New York: Columbia University Press, 1991.

Stefansson, Vilhjalmur. *The Adventure of Wrangel Island*. New York: The MacMillan Company, 1925.

Stefoff, Rebecca. *Women of the World: Women Travelers and Explorers*. New York: Oxford University Press, 1992.

Sterling, Dorothy, ed. *We Are Your Sisters: Black Women in the Nineteenth Century*. New York/London: W.W. Norton & Company, 1984.

Wylie, Betty Jane. *Reading Between the Lines; The Diaries of Women*. Toronto: Key Porter Books, 1995.

Yellin, Jean Fagan. *Harriet Jacobs: A Life*. New York: Basic Civitas Books, 2004.

LETTERS

Clode, Thomas (Sub-Protector of Aborigines, Port Augusta), 14 February, 1910. Cited as part of Human Rights and Equal Opportunity Commission (Australia), *Bringing Them Home—Report of the National Inquiry into the Separation of Aboriginal and Torres Strait Islander Children from Their Families*, April 1997.

ARCHIVES

Bury and Norwich Post Newspaper Archives: August 16, 1797; April 2, 1800; August 6, 1800.

Letter-Journals of Mary (Hayden) Russell and Captain Forman Marshall Mount, 1823-1824 (unpublished). In the collection of the Nantucket Historical Association.

The Papers of Ada Blackjack, in the Dartmouth College Library.

FILM, TELEVISION, RADIO

American Experience: Around the World in 72 Days. Written, produced, and directed by Christine Lesiak. PBS, 2005.

Great Lives, BBC Radio 4. "Mary Kingsley,"Program 10. Interview with Dea Burkett. Transcript available at: http://www.royalafricansociety.org/index.php?option=com_content&task=view&id=170&Itemid=166

The Incredible Journey of Mary Bryant. Directed by Peter Andrikidis. Written by Peter Berry. Granada Television, 2005.

Rabbit-Proof Fence. Directed by Phillip Noyce. Written by Christine Olsen. Rumbalara Films, 2002.

The Secret Life of Mrs. Beeton. Directed by Jon Jones. Written by Sarah Williams. British Broadcasting Corporation, 2006.

Vietnam: A Television History. Produced for WGBH TV, 1983. "Peace Is at Hand (1968-1973)," Episode 10. Written and produced by Martin Smith.

ACKNOWLEDGMENTS

For providing help in the creation of this book, heartfelt thanks to:

Doris Pilkington Garimara
Fred Whitehurst
Kim Tram
Hien Tram
Leslie Overton
Joanne King

PHOTO CREDITS

Page 1: *Sei Shonagon* by Uemura Shoen (上村松園, 1875-1949). Courtesy of Kyoto Journal.

Page 9: *Margaret Catchpole.* Courtesy of Colchester and Ipswich Museum Service.
Page 13: *Margaret attempting her escape.* Courtesy of Suffolk Record Office.
Page 14: *Notice of Margaret Catchpole's escape from prison,* c.1790, photographed for the Government Printing Office. Courtesy of Mitchell Library, State Library of New South Wales.

Page 27: *Perilous situation of whalemen,* 1861. Courtesy of the Library of Congress.

Page 43: *Portrait of Harriet Jacobs* courtesy of Jean Fagan Yellin.
Page 51: $100 reward poster published in *American Beacon,* Norfolk Virginia, July 4, 1835.

Page 61: Isabella Beeton (1836-65).
Page 69: Cover image of *Beeton's Book of Household Management: Comprising information for the Mistress, Housekeeper, Cook, Kitchen-Maid, Butler, Footman, Coachman, Valet, Upper and Under House-Maids, Maid-of-all-Work, Laundry-Maid, Nurse and Nurse-Maid, Monthly Wet and Sick Nurses, etc. etc. Also Sanitary, Media, & Legal Memoranda: with a History of the Origin, Properties, and Uses of all Things Connected with Home Life and Comfort,* published in 1861.

Page 77: Mary Kingsley © Royal Geographical Society. Courtesy of RGS Picture Library.

Page 95: *Nellie Bly* © H.J. Myers, 1890. Courtesy of the Library of Congress.

Page 117: *Daisy Ashford*. Courtesy of Mary Evans Picture Library.

Page 127: *Ada Blackjack*. Courtesy of Rauner Special Collections Library, Dartmouth College.
Page 133: *Ada Blackjack*. Courtesy of Rauner Special Collections Library, Dartmouth College.

Page 147: *Dang Thuy Tram*. Courtesy of Kim Tram Dang.

Page 159: *Doris Pilkington Garimara*. Courtesy of University of Queensland Press.